Joseph Salkeld

Classical Antiquities

With a Sketch of Ancient Mythology

Joseph Salkeld

Classical Antiquities
With a Sketch of Ancient Mythology

ISBN/EAN: 9783744694704

Printed in Europe, USA, Canada, Australia, Japan

Cover: Foto ©Thomas Meinert / pixelio.de

More available books at **www.hansebooks.com**

CLASSICAL ANTIQUITIES,

OR

A COMPENDIUM

OF

ROMAN AND GRECIAN

ANTIQUITIES;

WITH

A SKETCH OF ANCIENT MYTHOLOGY.

BY JOSEPH SALKELD.

NEW YORK:
HARPER & BROTHERS, PUBLISHERS,
FRANKLIN SQUARE.
1860.

PREFACE.

THIS work is designed as a manual of Classical Antiquities, and is divided into two parts : the first containing an account of the political institutions, religion, military and naval affairs, arts and sciences, manners, customs, &c., pertaining to the Romans ; and the second, those relating to the Grecians.

Most of the works in use, which treat of the Antiquities of these celebrated nations, are so copious and so intermingled with Greek or Latin quotations, that, though they may be highly valuable to the classical *scholar* as works of reference, they are rendered less useful to the classical *pupil*, as common text-books. There have, it is true, been published, in this country, one or two small volumes in which it is attempted to describe the Antiquities of the Romans, but these works are so contracted in matter as to be either partially or entirely deficient in many important subjects of which they profess to treat. The author has endeavored to adopt a medium course, by avoiding too great copiousness as well as a scanty conciseness of matter, and he trusts his treatise will be found sufficiently comprehensive for general use in academies and highschools, as well as in colleges.

In the prosecution of his undertaking, he has availed himself of every source of information within his reach, and he has freely borrowed whatever he thought adapted to his purpose. But in no case has he drawn from any source of questionable authority. In addition to consulting the classic authors themselves, he has profited from the writings of Kennet, Adam, Raper, Middleton, Arbuthnot, Gesner, Duncan, Potter, Barthelemi, (Travels of Anacharsis,) Cramer, Niebuhr, Burton, Mitford, Gillies, Rollin, Gibbon, and others.

To render the work more valuable, he has added a sketch of the Mythology of the Grecians and Romans.

The author has studied to make his work not only useful in *matter*, but also in *manner*. Most compilers of Grecian and Roman antiquities have overlooked a very important object, namely, a *systematic order* or *arrangement* of the subjects. The convenience and advantage of the regular arrangement of the subjects treated of in the present volume, will, it is thought, be readily admitted. especially by instructors and learners

Jan. 1844.

CONTENTS OF ROMAN ANTIQUITIES.

CHAPTER I.

GEOGRAPHY AND TOPOGRAPHY OF ROME.

CHAPTER II.

CIVIL GOVERNMENT AND POLITICAL ECONOMY OF ROME.

CHAPTER III.

MILITARY AND NAVAL AFFAIRS OF THE ROMANS.

CHAPTER IV.

RELIGION OF THE ROMANS.

CHAPTER V.

PUBLIC GAMES AND AMUSEMENTS OF THE ROMANS.

CHAPTER VI.

DOMESTIC AFFAIRS OF THE ROMANS.

CHAPTER VII.

ANTIQUITIES OF GREECE.

CHAPTER 1.

GEOGRAPHY AND TOPOGRAPHY.

CHAPTER II.

CIVIL GOVERNMENT AND POLITICAL ECONOMY OF THE ATHENIANS.

B

———

CHAPTER III.

CIVIL GOVERNMENT OF THE LACEDÆMONIANS.

———

CHAPTER IV

MILITARY AND NAVAL AFFAIRS OF THE GREEKS.

CHAPTER V.

RELIGION OF THE GREEKS.

CHAPTER VI.

PUBLIC GAMES AND AMUSEMENTS OF THE GREEKS.

CHAPTER VII.

DOMESTIC AFFAIRS OF THE GREEKS.

CHAPTER VIII.

TIME, MEASURES, WEIGHTS, AND MONEY OF THE GREEKS.

ANTIQUITIES OF ROME.

CHAPTER I.

GEOGRAPHY AND TOPOGRAPHY.

Section I.

A General Geographical View of the Roman Empire, its Boundaries, and Principal Divisions.

The dominion of Rome, which at first extended only over the city of the same name, afterward spread over a great portion of the then known world. The limits which the emperor Augustus set to the Roman empire, were the Atlantic Ocean on the west; the river Euphrates on the east; the rivers Danube and Rhine on the north; the cataracts of the Nile, the deserts of Africa, and Mount Atlas, on the south. This included the whole Mediterranean sea and the greater part of the world as known to the ancients. Some ad-

ditions were made to the empire beyond the
northern and eastern boundaries which had
been fixed by Augustus.

But the country of the Romans was more
generally limited to the whole of Italy, (*Italia,*)
which was subdivided into various states or
confederacies. The principal of these were,
1. Liguria; 2. Gallia Cisalpina; 3. Venetia,
including Histria and the Carni; 4. Etruria;
5. Umbria, and Picenum; 6. The Sabini, Æqui,
Marsi, Peligni, Vestini, Marrucini; 7. Roma;
8. Latium; 9. Campania; 10. Samnium, and
the Frentani; 11. Apulia, including Daunia
and Messapia or Iapygia; 12. Lucania; 13.
Brutii.

Italy was known by other names, as Hes-
peria, Ausonia, Œnotria, and Saturnia. The
northern part was called Gallia Cisalpina; the
middle, Italia Propria; and the south, Magna
Græcia, from its containing Greek colonies.

The principal mountains were *Alpes,* (the
Alps,) and *Apenninus,* (the Apennines.) The
principal rivers were the *Padus* or *Eridanus,*
(Po,) the *Tiber,* and the *Arnus,* (Arno.)

Sicilia, which was the largest and most
celebrated island in the Mediterranean sea,
was also called *Sicania,* and sometimes *Tri-
nacria,* from its having three promontories at
its three angles. On each of these promontories was a temple. Near the east end of the
island is the famous volcano Ætna. The
whirlpool of *Charybdis,* on the coast of Sicily

ın the Sicilian strait, and the promontory or
high rock of Scylla, opposite to it on the shore
of Italy, were proverbial among the ancients
as objects of terror to mariners, but are no
longer considered formidable.

Section II.

Rome.

The city of Rome, (*Roma,*) the capital of the
Roman Empire, was founded by Romulus, and
a colony from Alba Longa, 753 years before
Christ.   It was built upon seven hills, the Palatine, Capitoline, Quirinal, Aventine, Cœlian,
Viminal, and Esquiline.   It was situated on
the river Tiber, about sixteen miles from its
mouth.   The city was small and mean at first,
occupying only the Palatine hill; but at the
time of its greatest magnificence it covered a
space, within its suburbs, of fifty miles.   The
gates of Rome at the time of the death of
Romulus, were three or four; in the time of
Augustus, thirty-seven; at which time, the
circumference of the walls was more than
thirteen miles.

Rome was sometimes called the seven-hill-
ed city, (*septicollis.*)   Other hills were added as
the city became enlarged.

The Capitol, (*Capitolium,*) was a celebrated

temple and citadel on the Tarpeian rock or Capitoline Mount. It was planned by Tarquinius Priscus, begun by Servius Tullius, and finished by Tarquinius Superbus. It was constructed upon four acres of ground; the front was adorned with three rows of pillars, and the other sides with two. The ascent to it from the ground was by a hundred steps. The magnificence and richness of this temple are almost incredible. All the consuls successively made donations to the Capitol; and Augustus bestowed upon it, at one time, two thousand pounds weight of gold. Its thresholds were made of brass, and its roof was gold. It was adorned with vessels and shields of solid silver, with golden chariots, &c. It was burnt and rebuilt three different times. The last time it was restored by Domitian, who made it more grand and magnificent than any of his predecessors. The edifice of the Capitol was in the form of a square. It contained three temples, consecrated respectively to Jupiter, Juno, and Minerva. The temple of Jupiter was in the middle; of Minerva, on the right; and of Juno, on the left. The Capitol was the highest part of the city, and strongly fortified.

The Pantheon, now called the Rotunda, or temple of all the gods, was built by Agrippa, in the time of Augustus, and its solid construction promises it a duration for many centuries yet to come. Some time after its erection it was struck with lightning and partly destroyed; but was repaired by Adrian. The walls in the inside are either solid marble or incrusted. The front on the outside was covered with brazen plates gilded; and the top, with silver plates. The gate was of brass of extraordinary work and size.

The temple of Apollo, built by Augustus on the Palatine hill, contained a public library, where authors, and particularly poets, used to recite their compositions.

The temple of Janus, built by Numa, had two brazen gates, one on each side, to be open in time of war, and shut in time of peace.

The temple of Saturn was appropriated for the public treasury, in which all the public registers were preserved.

There were also temples of Juno, Mars, Venus, Minerva, Neptune, &c., of Romulus, of Fortune, Concord, Peace, &c.

The Odeum was a building where musicians rehearsed, or privately exercised themselves before they appeared on the stage.

The Theatres of Pompey, of Marcellus, and the wooden one of Marcus Scaurus, were immense and magnificent structures. The last was capable of containing eighty thousand persons.

The Colisæum, built by Vespasian and Titus as an Amphitheatre, was of an oval form, and could contain eighty-seven thousand spectators. It was five hundred and fifty feet in length, four hundred and eighty in breadth, and one hundred and fifty-eight in height. It was surrounded to the top by a portico supported by eighty arches and divided into four stories.

The *Circus Maximus* was first built by Tarquinius Priscus, and afterwards, at different times, magnificently adorned. It was situated between the Palatine and Aventine hills, and was of an oblong circular form. It was seven hundred and thirty yards long, and about one-third as wide, having a circumference of a mile, and capable of containing one hundred and fifty thousand spectators, or, according to Pliny, two hundred and fifty thousand.

The principal public place in the city was the *Forum*. This was a large open space of oblong shape, where the people held their assemblies, and where justice was administered and public business transacted. It was surrounded in its whole extent with arched porticoes which enclosed spacious halls adorned with other porticoes and columns. There were also various *Foræ* or market places where commodities were sold.

The *Campus Martius* was a large plain without the city along the river Tiber, where the athletic exercises and sports of the Roman youth were practised. It was adorned with many noble structures and monuments.

The Porticoes were among the most splendid ornaments of Rome. The Columns or pillars gave also additional embellishment to the city. The most remarkable of these were those of Trajan and Antonius Pius. Trajan's pillar was erected in the middle of his Forum, and was composed of twenty-four great blocks of marble, but so skilfully cemented as to seem but one. Its height is one hundred and twenty-eight feet. It is about twelve feet in diameter at the bottom, and ten at the top. It has in the inside one hundred and eighty-five winding steps for ascending, and forty windows for the admission of light. The whole pillar is incrusted with marble, on which are represented the warlike exploits of that emperor and his army. On the top was a colossal statue of Trajan.

The pillar of Antonius was erected to him by the senate after his death. It is one hundred and seventy-six feet high, the steps of its ascent one hundred and six, the windows fifty-six. The sculpture and other ornaments are much of the same kind with those of Trajan's pillar; but the work far inferior. Both of these pillars are still standing, but instead of the statues of the emperors, the statue of St. Peter has been erected on Trajan's pillar, and of St. Paul on that of Antonius, by order of Pope Sextus V.

The *Milliarium Aureum* was a gilded pillar in the Forum where all the military ways or roads terminated.

Among the many ornaments of the city

were the triumphal Arches, (*arcus triumphales,*) erected in honor of illustrious generals, who had gained signal victories in war. They were generally very magnificent, built of the finest marble, of a square figure, with a large arched gate in the middle and two small ones on each side, adorned with columns and statues and various figures of sculpture.

Trophies (*trophœa*) were spoils taken from the enemy and fixed upon any thing as signs or monuments of victory, erected usually on the spot where it was gained, and consecrated to some divinity, with an inscription.

The Aqueducts, of which there were about twenty; the Bridges, of which there were eight; and even the Sewers (*cloacæ*) for draining off the filth of the city into the Tiber, were all built at a great expense and curiously adorned. Some of the Baths (*thermæ*) were built with astonishing magnificence.

The Public Ways (*viæ*) were perhaps the greatest of all the Roman works, being made with amazing labor and expense to a great distance from the city. They were generally paved with flint. The Appian way in several places remains entire unto this day, though constructed more than two thousand years ago.

Everywhere around Rome are still to be seen magnificent ruins of many of the public buildings above noticed, Egyptian obelisks, blocks of oriental granite, and ancient private buildings.

The following is a part of the summary catalogue of the different buildings, monuments, and principal curiosities of Rome, as contained in the notice of Aurelius Victor. Senate Houses of the city 4; Public Libraries 28; Great Obelisks 6; Smaller Obelisks 42; Highways 29; Campi 8; Bridges 8; Forums 18; Basilics 11; Public Hot Baths 12; Aqueducts 20; Capitols 2; Amphitheatres 3; Colossal Statues 2; Provision Markets 2; Theatres 3; Schools for exercising in the Games 5; Naumachiæ (places for shows of sea-fights) 5; Nymphea (buildings adorned with statues of the nymphs, and abounding in fountains and waterfalls) 11; Statues of brazen Horses overlaid with gilt 24; Statues of Horses made of ivory 94; Marble Arches 36; Gates 37; Blocks of Houses 424; Insulated Houses (i. e. houses having no other house joined to it, but a street on every side; such were great men's houses) 46,602; Baths 856.

CHAPTER II.

CIVIL GOVERNMENT AND POLITICAL ECONOMY
OF ROME.

SECTION I.

Inhabitants of Rome.

THE inhabitants of Rome were divided by Romulus into three Tribes, and each tribe into ten *curiæ.* The number of tribes was afterwards increased by degrees to thirty-five. The number of *curiæ* always remained the same.

The people were at first divided into two ranks, (*ordines,*) Patricians, (*patricii,*) and Plebeians, (*plebs* or *populus.*) Afterwards a third order was added, called *Equites,* (knights;) and slavery being introduced formed another class. There were therefore in all four classes. The number of inhabitants of the city in its most flourishing state was about four millions.

The Patrician order was composed of those families whose ancestors had been members of the senate. They were considered noble, because members of their family had filled high offices. They enjoyed many distinguished privileges from which the other ranks were excluded.

The Knights or Equestrian order arose out of an institution of Romulus, who chose from each of the three tribes one hundred young men, the most distinguished for their rank and other accomplishments, who should serve on horseback, and whose assistance he might use for guarding his person. The number was afterwards increased to six hundred by an addition of three hundred chosen from the Albans. Afterwards this number was more than doubled; and under Servius Tullius there were eighteen hundred *Equites.*

The *Equites* were chosen promiscuously from the Patricians and Plebeians by the Censor. The age requisite was about eighteen years and the fortune four hundred *sestertia,* (14,351 dollars.)

The badges or mark of distinction of the *Equites* were,—1. A horse presented them at the public expense; 2. A golden ring; 3. A narrow strip of purple sewed on the breast of their tunic, (*angustus clavus;*) and 4. A separate place at the public shows.

The office of the *Equites* at first was only to serve in the army; but afterwards also to act as judges or jurymen, and to farm the public revenues.

A great degree of splendor was added to the Equestrian order by a procession (*transvectio*) which they made through the city every year on the 15th day of July, from the temple of Honor, or of Mars, without the city, to the

Capitol; riding on horseback, with wreaths of olive on their heads, dressed in their *Togæ palmatæ*, or *trabeæ* of a scarlet color, and bearing in their hands the military ornaments which they had received from their general as a reward for their valor. At this time it was not allowable to cite them before a court of justice.

Every fifth year, when this procession was made, the *Equites* rode up to the Censor seated in his curule chair before the Capitol, and dismounting, led along their horses before him, and in this manner they were reviewed. If any *Eques* was corrupt in his morals, or had diminished his fortune, or even had not taken proper care of his horse, the Censor ordered him to sell his horse, and thus he was considered to be degraded from the Equestrian order; but those whom the Censor approved, were ordered to lead along their horses.

The Plebeian order, which formed the mass of the people, was composed of the lowest class of freemen, or as now termed, ' the common people.' Those who lived in the country were called '*Plebs rustica*,' and were the more respectable; those who resided in the city, as merchants, mechanics, &c., were called ' *Plebs urbana*.' Many of these latter followed no trade, but were supported by the public and private largesses. There were leading men among them, kept in pay by the seditious magistrates, who would stimulate them to the most daring outrages. The turbulence of the common people of Rome—the natural effect of idleness and unbounded licentiousness—is justly reckoned among the chief causes of the ruin of the republic. Trade and manufactures being considered as servile employments, they had no encouragement to industry; and the numerous spectacles which were exhibited, particularly the shows of gladiators, served but to increase their natural ferocity. Hence they were always ready to join in any conspiracy against the state.

That the Patricians and Plebeians might be connected together by the strictest bonds, Romulus ordained that every Plebeian should choose from the Patricians any one he pleased as his Patron or protector, whose Client he was called. The Patron was bound to protect his Client, to relieve him in distress, to appear for him in court, to expound the law to him, and to assist him on all necessary occasions. On the other hand, the Client was obliged to be dutiful and obedient to his Patron, to promote his honor, and to serve him with his fortune, or even with his life, if required. There was a mutual bond between the Patron and the Client that neither should bring an accusation or bear witness against the other, or give sentence in court against him or in favor of his enemies. The duties of the Patron towards his Client were more sacred than those towards his own kindred. Whoever trespassed against

C

his clients was guilty of treason, and might be slain by any one with impunity.

In after times, even cities and whole nations placed themselves under the protection of illustrious Roman families.

Those whose ancestors or who themselves had borne any Curule magistracy; that is, had been Consul, Prætor, Censor, or Curule Ædile, were called *nobiles*, and had the right of making waxen images of themselves, which were kept with great care by their posterity in the courts of their houses, enclosed in wooden cases, and brought out only on solemn occasions and at funerals of the family, when they were carried before them.

Men became slaves among the Romans by being taken in war, by way of punishment, or by being born in a state of servitude. Those enemies who voluntarily laid down their arms and surrendered themselves, retained their rights of freedom, and were called ‘ *dedititii*.’ Those taken in the field or in the storming of cities were sold at auction (‘ *sub corona*’ because they wore a crown when sold) or (‘ *sub hasta*’ because a spear was set up where the auctioneer stood.) They were called *servi* or *mancipia*. There was a constant market for slaves at Rome. Those who dealt in this trade (*mangones*, or *venalitii*) brought them from various countries. The seller was bound to promise for the soundness of his slaves, and not to conceal their faults. Hence they were generally exposed for sale marked; and they carried a scroll hanging at their necks, on which their good and bad qualities were specified. If the seller gave a false account he was bound to make up the loss, or to take back the slave.

Free-born citizens could not sell themselves for slaves. Fathers might sell their children for slaves, but these did not on that account entirely lose the right of citizens; for when freed from their slavery, they were held as *Ingenui*, not *Libertini*.* The same was the case with insolvent debtors who were given up as slaves to their creditors. Criminals, who were reduced to slavery by way of punishment, were first deprived of citizenship and liberty, and were called slaves of punishment, (*servi pœnæ.*)

The children of any female slave became the slaves of her master. There was no regular marriage among slaves, but their connection was termed *contubernium*. The whole company of slaves in one house was called *familia*, and the proprietor, *dominus*.

Slaves not only did all domestic services, but were likewise employed in various trades and manufactures. Such as had a genius for it, were sometimes instructed in literature and the liberal arts. Some of these were sold at a great price.

Slaves were promoted according to their

* See Sect. II.

behavior, as from being a drudge or mean slave in town, to be an overseer in the country [*villicus.*]

Among the Romans, masters had an absolute power over their slaves. They might scourge or put them to death at pleasure. This right was exercised with so great cruelty that laws were made at different times to restrain it. The lash was the common punishment, but for some crimes they were branded in the forehead; and sometimes compelled to carry a piece of wood round their necks, wherever they went; which was called *furca*, and the slave who carried it, *furcifur*. Slaves by way of punishment were often shut up in a workhouse, (*ergastulum*,) where they were obliged to turn a mill for grinding corn. When slaves were beaten, they were suspended with a weight tied to their feet, that they might not move them. When punished capitally, they were commonly crucified; but this kind of punishment was prohibited under the Christian emperor Constantine.

If the master of a family was slain at his own house, and the murderer not discovered, all his domestic slaves were liable to be put to death. Slaves were not esteemed as persons, but as things; and might be transferred from one owner to another, like any other effects. They could not appear as witnesses in a court of justice, nor make a will, nor inherit any thing, nor serve as soldiers, unless first made free. They had a certain allowance granted them for their sustenance, (*dimensium,*) commonly four or five pecks of grain a month, and five *denarii** in money. What they spared of this, or procured by any other means, with their master's consent, was called their *pecu lium.* This money they could put out at interest, or purchase with it a slave for themselves, from whose labors they might make profit. In this way they often purchased their freedom.

At certain times slaves were allowed the greatest freedom, as at the feast of Saturn in the month of December, when they were served at table by their masters. The number of slaves in Rome and throughout Italy was very great. Some rich individuals are said to have had several thousands.

Slaves were anciently freed in three ways,— 1. *Per Censum,* when a slave by his master's knowledge or order had his name inserted in the Censor's roll.—2. *Per vindictam,* when a master took his slave to the Prætor or Consul and said, "I desire that this man be free according to the custom of the Romans;" and the officer, if he approved, putting a rod (*vindicta*) on the head of the slave, pronounced, "I say that this man is free after the manner of the Romans." Then the lictor,† or the

* A *denarius* is about 14 or 15 cents.

† The *lictors* were persons taken from the lowest classes to go before magistrates and attend to their orders.

master, turning him round in a circle and giving him a blow on the cheek, let him go, signifying that leave was granted him to go where he pleased.—3. *Per testamentum*, when a master gave his slaves their liberty by his will.

Anciently the condition of all freed slaves was the same; they obtained the freedom of the city with their liberty. But in later times laws were made to check the license of manumitting slaves. When freed, they were presented with a white robe and a ring by their master. They then assumed a *prænomen* and prefixed the name of their patron to their own. So foreigners, when admitted to the freedom of the city, assumed the name of that person by whose favor they had obtained it. If a freedman died intestate without heirs, the patron succeeded to his effects.

Slaves when made free were called *liberti* and *libertini;—liberti* in relation to their masters; and *libertini* in relation to free-born citizens.

Section II.

Names of the Romans, Gentes, Familiæ, &c.

The Romans were divided into various clans, (*gentes*,) and each clan or *gens* into several families, (*familiæ*.) Those of the same *gens* were called *gentiles*, and those of the same family, *agnati*, to distinguish them from *cognati*, relations only by the mother's side. Anciently the Patricians only were said to have a *gens*. But when the Plebeians obtained the right of intermarriage they also received the rights of *gentes*.

To mark the different *gentes* and *familiæ*, and to distinguish individuals of the same family, the Romans had commonly three names; the *prænomen*, *nomen*, and *cognomen*. The *prænomen* was put first, and marked the individual. It was commonly written with one letter, as *A.* for *Aulus ; C.* for *Caius ;* sometimes with two letters, as *Ap.* for *Appius; Cn.* for *Cneius.* The *nomen* was put after the *prænomen* and marked the *gens*, and commonly ended in *ius*, as *Cornelius, Julius.* The *cognomen* was put last and marked the *familia*, as Cicero, Cæsar. Sometimes there was a fourth name, called the *agnomen*, added for some illustrious action or remarkable event. Thus Scipio was named *Africanus*, from the conquest of Carthage and Africa ; and on a similar account his brother Lucius was named *Asiaticus.* These three names were not always used, commonly but two, and sometimes only one, the *cognomen* or surname. But in speaking to any one, the *prænomen* was generally used as being peculiar to citizens, for slaves had no *prænomen.*

The surnames were derived from various circumstances, as from some quality of the mind, as Cato from wisdom, (*catus*, wise,) or habit of the body, &c., as Crassus, Macer.

The *prænomen* used to be given to boys on the ninth day, which was called *dies lustricus,* 'the day of purification,' when certain religious ceremonies were performed. The eldest son of the family usually received the *prænomen* of the father: the rest were named from their uncles or other relations. When there was only one daughter in the family she was called from the name of the *gens;* thus, *Tullia,* the daughter of Cicero; *Julia,* the daughter of Cæsar; and they retained the same name after they were married. When there were two daughters the elder was called *Major* and the other *Minor,* as Cornelia Major, Cornelia Minor. If there were more than two they were distinguished by their number; thus, *Prima, Secunda,* &c., or more genteelly, *Tertilla, Quartilla,* &c.

Those children were called *liberi,* ' free,' who had the liberty of doing what they pleased. Those born of parents who had been always free were called *ingenui.* Slaves made free were called *liberti,* in relation to their masters, and *libertini,* in relation to free-born citizens.*

* See page 27.

Magistrates.

The Roman magistrates were variously divided into *ordinary* and *extraordinary, greater* and *less, curule* and *not curule, patrician* and *plebeian, city* and *provincial magistrates.*

The *magistratus ordinarii* were those who were created at stated times, and were constantly in the republic ; the *extraordinarii* not so. The *magistratus majores* were the consuls, prætors, and censors of the *ordinary* kind, and the dictator, master of the horse, the interrex, the prefect of the city, &c., of the extraordinary kind. The *magistratus minores* were the tribunes of the people, the ædiles and quæstors. The *magistratus curules* were those who had the right of using the *sella curulis* or ' chair of state.' These were the dictator, the consuls, prætors, censors, and curule ædiles. All the rest who had not that right were called *non curules.* This *sella curulis* was made of ivory, or adorned with it. The magistrates sat on it in their tribunal on all solemn occasions.

In the beginning of the republic the magistrates were chosen only from the Patricians, but afterwards also from the Plebeians, except the interrex alone.

There was a certain age fixed for enjoying

the different offices, but it is not fully ascertained what that age was, in all cases. It is certain, however, that the prætorship used to be enjoyed two years after the ædileship, and that the consulship could not be held by any person before he had arrived at the age of forty-three. From Cicero we may infer that the years appointed for the different offices were, for the quæstorship, thirty-one; for the prætorship, forty; and for the consulship, forty-three.

All magistrates were obliged, within five days after entering upon the duties of their office, to swear that they would observe the laws; and after the expiration of their office they might be brought to trial if they had done any thing amiss.

Rome was at first governed by kings, (*reges*,) not of absolute power, nor hereditary, but limited and elective. They had no legislative authority, and could neither make war nor peace without the concurrence of the senate and people. The kings were also priests, and had the chief direction of sacred things. Their badges were the *trabea*, a white robe adorned with stripes of purple; or the *toga prætexta*, a white robe fringed with purple: *a golden crown, an ivory sceptre*, the *sella curulis*, and *twelve lictors* with the *fasces* and *secures*, i. e. carrying each of them a bundle of rods with an axe placed in the middle of them.

When there was a vacancy in the throne

(*interregnum,*) the senators shared the government and appointed one of their number to have the chief direction of affairs, with the title of *interrex*, for the space of five days; and after him another and another in succession till a king was elected. Afterwards, under the republic, an *interrex* was created to hold the elections, when there were no consuls or dictator; which happened either by their sudden death or when the tribunes of the people hindered the election by their intervention.

The regal government subsisted at Rome for two hundred and forty-three years under seven kings: *Romulus, Numa Pompilius, Tullus Hostilius, Ancus Martius, Tarquinius Priscus, Servius Tullius,* and *L. Tarquinius,* surnamed *Superbus* from his behavior: all of whom except the last so reigned that they are justly thought to have laid the foundations of the Roman greatness. Tarquin being universally detested for his tyranny and cruelty, was expelled the city on account of the violence offered by his son Sextus to Lucretia, a noble lady, the wife of Collatinus. This revolution was effected by means of L. Junius Brutus. The haughtiness and cruelty of Tarquin inspired the Romans with the greatest aversion to regal government, which they retained ever afterwards.

After the expulsion of the kings, A. U.* 244, two supreme magistrates were annually crea-

* A. U., that is, *anno urbis,* the year of the city.

ted with equal authority, who were called
Consules, (consuls.) Their badges were the
same as those of the kings except the crown,
namely, the *toga prætexta, sella curulis, scipio
eburneus*, (the ivory sceptre,) and *twelve lictors*
with the *fasces* and *secures*. They had nearly
the same power as the kings, but this was diminished by the creation of the tribunes of
the people, and still more afterwards by the
emperors.

The consuls were at the head of the whole
republic. All other magistrates were subject
to them except the tribunes of the people.
They assembled the people and the senate, laid
before them what they pleased, and executed
their decrees. The laws which they proposed
and had passed, were commonly called by
their names. They received all letters from
the governors of provinces, from foreign kings
and states, and gave audience to ambassadors.
The year was named after them. He who
had the most suffrages was called *consul prior*,
and his name was marked first in the calendar. He also presided at the election of magistrates for the next year.

Every one went out of the way, uncovered
his head, dismounted from horseback, or rose
up to the consuls as they passed by.

In time of war, the consuls possessed supreme command. They levied soldiers and
provided for them, and appointed most of the
military officers.

In dangerous conjunctures the consuls were armed with absolute power by the solemn decree of the senate that " *they* (the consuls) *hould see that the republic receives no harm.*"

The consuls were usually elected about the end of July or the beginning of August. From the time of their election to the first of January, when they entered upon their office, they were called *Consules designati,* ' consuls elect.' This interval was made so long that they might have time to become acquainted with what pertained to their office ; and that inquiry might be made whether they had gained their election by bribery. If they were convicted of that crime upon trial, they were deprived of consulship, fined, and declared ineligible to any office.

On the first day of January the senate and people waited on the new consuls at their houses, whence being conducted with great pomp (*processus consularis*) to the capitol, they offered up their vows, and sacrificed, each of them, an ox to Jupiter, and then began their office by holding the senate.

Before any one could be made consul it was requisite to have gone through the inferior offices of *quæstor, ædile, and prætor.*

Those who had been consuls were called *consulares,* ' men of consular dignity.'

The name of *Prætor* was anciently common to all the magistrates. But when the consuls, being engaged in almost continual wars, could not attend to the administration of justice, a magistrate was created for that purpose, to whom the name of *Prætor* was therefore appropriated. The prætor was next in dignity to the consuls, and was created at the *Comitia centuriata* with the same auspices as the con suls, whence he was called their colleague. When, on account of the number of foreigners who flocked to Rome, one prætor was not sufficient, another prætor was added to administer justice to them, or between citizens and them. He was called *prætor peregrinus.* The two prætors, after their election, decided by lot which of the two jurisdictions each should exercise. The prætor who administered justice only between citizens (*prætor urbanus*) was considered more honorable. In the absence of the consuls he supplied their place. He presided in the assemblies of the people, and might on some occasions convene the senate. On account of his important office, he was not allowed to be absent from the city above ten days.

The power of the prætor in the administration of justice, was expressed in these three words, *do, dico, addico.* By *do,* he gave the form of a writ for trying and redressing a particular wrong complained of, and appointed judges or a jury to judge in the cause ; by *dico,* he pronounced sentence ; and by *addico,* he adjudged the goods of the debtor to the creditor. The days on which the prætor administered justice were called *dies fasti*, and those days on which it was unlawful to administer justice, *dies nefasti*.

When the *prætor urbanus* entered upon his office, after having sworn to the observance of the laws, he published an edict (*edictum*) or system of rules, according to which he was to administer justice for that year. The summoning of any one to appear in court was also called *edictum*. Other magistrates, however, published their edicts, as well as the prætor.

The prætor was attended by two lictors in the city who went before him with the *fasces*, and by six lictors without the city. He wore the *toga prætexta*, which he assumed as the consuls did on the first day of his office, after having offered up vows in the capitol. When he heard causes, he sat in the *Forum* or *Comitium* on a *tribunal*, which was a kind of stage or scaffold, in which was placed the *sella curulis* of the prætor; and a sword and spear (*gladius et hasta*) were set upright before him. The *judices* or jury sat on some lower seats, as also did the witnesses, advocates, &c. The clerks (*scribæ*) recorded his proceeding; and the criers (*accensi*) summoned persons, and proclaimed the hour at certain times of the day.

The number of prætors increased as the empire extended more widely, but two only of the number remained in the city. The rest were sent to the provinces

The prætors administered justice only in private or less causes, but in public or important causes, the people either judged themselves, or appointed one or more persons to preside at the trial, who were called *Quæsitores*, and whose authority lasted only till the trial was over.

The *Censores* were two magistrates first created A. U. 312, for taking an account of the number of the people, and the value of their fortunes, and especially to inspect the morals of the citizens. They were elected every five years, but their power continued only a year and a half. They had the same badges of honor as the consuls, except the lictors. They were usually chosen from the most respectable persons of consular dignity. Their power in time became very great. The title of Censor was esteemed more honorable even than that of consul, and it was reckoned the chief ornament of nobility to be sprung from a censorian family.

The censors took the *census* in the Campus Martius. Seated in their curule chairs, and attended by their clerks and other officers, they ordered the citizens divided into their classes and centuries, and also into their tribes, to be called before them by a herald, and to give an account of their fortunes, family, &c. At the same time they reviewed the senate and equestrian order, supplied the vacant places in both, and inflicted various marks of disgrace on those who deserved it, such as excluding a senator from the senate-house; depriving a knight of his public horse; and removing a citizen from a more honorable to a less honorable tribe, or depriving him of the privileges of a Roman citizen, except liberty.

The censors divided the citizens into classes and centuries, according to their fortunes. They added new tribes to the old when it was deemed expedient. They also had charge of the public works, paving the streets, making roads, bridges, aqueducts, keeping the temples and public edifices in repair, letting out the public lands and taxes, and taking care that private persons should not occupy what belonged to the public.

The power of the censors did not extend to public crimes, or to such things as came under the cognizance of the civil magistrate and were punishable by law; but only to matters of a private nature, and of less importance, as if any one did not cultivate his ground properly, if an *eques* did not take proper care of his horse, if one lived too long unmarried, or contracted debt without cause, if one had not behaved with sufficient bravery in war, or was of dissolute morals, and, above all, if a person had violated his oath. The accused were usually permitted to make their defence. The sentence of the censors (*animadversio censoria*) affected only the rank and character of persons, and was called *ignominia*, but this was

D

not fixed and unalterable, for the next cen
sors, or the verdict of a jury, or the suffrages
of the people, might remove it.

No one could be elected a second time to
the office of censor; and if one of the censors
died, his surviving colleague was obliged to
resign his office.

The review (*census*) of the people by the
censors, took place every five years. After it
was finished, an expiatory sacrifice was made
of a sow, a sheep, and a bull, which were
carried round the whole assembly and then
slain, and thus the people were said to be purified, (*lustrati,*) and hence the word *lustrum*
(purification) came to denote a period of five
years.

The plebeians being oppressed by the patricians on account of debt, made a secession to
a mountain, afterwards called *Mons Sacer,*
three miles from Rome, A. U. 260; nor could
they be prevailed on to return, till they obtained from the patricians a remission of debts
for those who were insolvent, and liberty to
such as had been given up to their creditors;
and likewise that the plebeians should have
proper magistrates of their own to protect
their rights, whose persons should be sacred
and inviolable. These magistrates were called
Tribuni. At first five were created, but afterwards ten. They were chosen indiscriminately
from the plebeians, and no patrician could be
made tribune unless first adopted into a ple-

beian family. They had no external mark of dignity except a kind of beadle (*viator*) who went before them.

The power of the tribunes was at first very limited. It consisted in hindering, not in acting; and was expressed by the word *veto*, "I forbid it." But in process of time they increased their influence to such a degree, that under the pretext of defending the rights of the people, they did almost whatever they pleased. They hindered the collection of tribute, the enlisting of soldiers, and the creation of magistrates; which latter they did at one time for five years. They could put a negative upon all the decrees of the senate and ordinances of the people, and by a single *veto* could arrest the proceedings of all magistrates. If any one injured a tribune in word or in deed, he was held accursed, and his property was confiscated. Under the sanction of this law they carried their power to an extravagant height. The only effectual method of resisting their power, was to procure one of their number to put a negative on the proceedings of the rest; but he who did it might afterwards be brought by his colleagues to trial before the people.

The *Ædiles* were named from their care of the public buildings, (*ædes.*) They were either plebeian or curule. Two *ædiles plebeii* were first created at the same time with the tribunes **of the people,** to be their assistants, and to determine certain less causes which the tribunes committed to them. Two *ædiles curules* were created from the patricians to perform certain public games. These wore the *toga prætexta*, had the right of images, and a more honorable place of giving their opinion in the senate. Their office was to take care of the city, its public buildings, temples, theatres, baths, porticoes, aqueducts, roads, &c., also of private buildings, lest they should become ruinous, and deform the city, or occasion danger to passengers. They likewise took care of provisions, markets, taverns, &c.; they inspected things which were exposed to sale in the Forum; and if they were not good, they caused them to be thrown into the Tiber; they broke unjust weights and measures, and examined plays that were to be brought upon the stage. The plebeian ædiles kept the decrees of the senate and the ordinances of the people in the temple of Ceres, and afterwards in the treasury.

The *Quæstores* were appointed by the people to take charge of the public revenues, and were at first two in number, but were afterwards increased to eight; but two only remained at Rome, called *quæstores urbani*. These two city quæstors had the care of the treasury, which was kept in the temple of Saturn; they received and expended the public money, exacted fines, kept the military standards, entertained foreign ambassadors, and took charge of the funerals of those who were buried at the public expense.

The office of the provincial quæstors (*quæstores provinciales*) was to attend the consuls or prætors into their provinces, to take care that provisions and pay were furnished to the army, to keep the money deposited by the soldiers, to exact the taxes and tribute of the empire, to sell the spoils taken in war, and to return an account of every thing to the treasury.

The quæstors were not attended by lictors nor *viatores*.

The quæstorship was the first step of preferment to the higher offices, and of admission in the senate.

Section IV.

Other Magistrates.

The *Dictator* was a magistrate with absolute power, appointed on extraordinary occasions, or in cases of imminent danger from pestilence, sedition, or foreign enemies. His power was supreme, both in peace and war. He could raise and disband armies; he could determine on the life and fortunes of citizens without consulting the people or senate. From his decision there was no appeal. When he was created, all other magistrates, except the tribunes of the people, resigned their authority. His office continued only for six months; but he usually resigned his command whenever he had effected the business for which he had been created. He was not permitted to go out of Italy, nor to ride on horseback without asking permission of the people. But the principal check against a dictator's abuse of power was, that he might be called to an account for his conduct when he resigned his office.

The dictator was not created by the suffrages of the people as the other magistrates; but one of the consuls, by order of the senate, named as dictator whatever person of consular dignity he thought proper after having taken the auspices, usually in the dead of the night.

When a dictator was created he immediately nominated a master of horse, (*Magister Equitum*,) usually from those of consular or prætorian rank, whose office was to command the cavalry, and to execute the orders of the dictator.

The *Decemviri* were ten men created A. U. 303, from the patricians, with supreme power to draw up a code of laws, all the other magistrates having first resigned their offices. They administered justice to the people each every tenth day, and behaved at first with great moderation. They proposed ten tables of laws, which were ratified by the people at the *comitia centuriata*. As two other tables seemed to be wanting, decemvirs were again created, for another year, to make them. But these new magistrates acting tyrannically, and wishing to retain their command beyond the legal time, were at last forced to resign, chiefly on account of the base passion of one of the number, Appius Claudius, for Virginia, a virgin of plebeian rank, who was slain by her father to prevent her falling into the decemvir's hands. The decemvirs all perished either in prison or in banishment.

The *Tribuni Militum*, or military tribunes, had consular power in public affairs, and mediated between the patricians and plebeians at a time when they could not agree about an election of consuls.

The provinces of the people were governed by Pro-consuls and Pro-prætors, to whom were joined quæstors and lieutenants, (*legati.*) The office of a *legatus* was very honorable.

After the death of Julius Cæsar, A. U. 710, Octavius, (who was afterwards called Augustus,) Antony, and Lepidus, shared between them the provinces of the republic, and exercised absolute power under the title of *Triumviri*. After this, Augustus, A. U. 723, became sole master of the Roman empire, and ruled it under the title of Prince or Emperor, (*Princeps* or *Imperator.*) The title of *Imperator* (by which the chief magistrate was called) continued till the downfall of the empire. The emperors made numerous alterations and

appointments in the offices, but nearly all the
authority of different magistrates was concen-
trated in the emperor.   Among the new offices
instituted by the emperors, were the *Præfecti*
and *Procuratores*.   The *præfectus urbi* was the
governor of the city; the *præfectus prætorio*
was the commander of the emperor's body-
guards; the *præfectus annonæ* had the charge
of procuring corn in times of scarcity; the
præfectus militaris ærarii had charge of the
public fund; the *præfectus classis* was the admiral of the fleet; the *præfectus vigilum* was
the officer who commanded the soldiers that
were appointed to watch the city.

The *Procurator* in each province managed
the affairs of the revenue.

Section V.

Public Assemblies.

An assembly of the whole Roman people to
give their vote about any subject was called
comitia.   When a part of the people only was
assembled it was usually called *consilium*.   In
the *Comitia*, every thing which came under
the power of the people was transacted; magistrates were elected, and laws passed, particularly concerning the declaration of war
and the concluding of peace.   Persons guilty

of certain crimes were also tried in the *comitia*. The *comitia* were always summoned by some magistrate who presided in them.

There were three kinds of *Comitia*, the *Curiata*, instituted by Romulus; the *Centuriata*, instituted by Servius Tullius; and the *Tributa*, introduced by the tribunes of the people. The two former could not be held without taking the auspices, nor without the authority of the senate; but the *Tributa* might. The *comitia* for creating magistrates were usually held in the *Campus Martius;* but for making laws and for holding trials, sometimes in the forum, and sometimes in the capitol.

In the *comitia*, as well as in the senate, nothing could be done before the rising nor after the setting of the sun. The days on which the *comitia* could be held were called *dies comitiales*.

In the *Comitia. Curiata*, the people gave their votes, divided into thirty *curiæ;* and what a majority of them (that is, sixteen) determined, was said to be the order of the people. At first there were no other *comitia* but the *curiata*, and therefore every thing of importance was determined by them. The kings and afterwards the consuls presided, and directed every thing which came before them. The part of the forum where they assembled was called the *Comitium*. Those citizens only had a right to vote at the *comitia curiata* who lived in the city and were includ-

E

ed in some *curia* or parish. A law made by
the people divided into *curiæ* was called *lex
curiata*. After the institution of the *comitia
centuriata* and *tributa*, the *comitia curiata* were
more rarely assembled, and that only for passing certain laws, the creation of the *Curiæ
Maximus*, (the president of the *curiæ*,) and for
conferring military command on magistrates.

The principal *comitia* were the *centuriata*,
in which the people divided into the centuries
of their classes gave their votes, and what a
majority of centuries decreed was considered
as finally determined. These *comitia* were
held according to the *census* instituted by Servius Tullius. This census was a numbering of
the people with a valuation of their fortunes.
All the Roman citizens, both in town and
country, upon oath made an estimate of their
fortunes, and publicly declared that estimate
to the Censor ; they told also the names of
their wives and children, the number of their
slaves and freedmen, their own age and that
of their children, and if any gave a false account their goods were confiscated, and themselves scourged and sold for slaves. Then
according to the valuation of their estates he
divided all the citizens into six classes, and
each class into a certain number of centuries.
At first a century contained a hundred, but
not so afterwards.

The first class consisted of those whose estates in lands and effects were worth at least

one hundred thousand *asses* or pounds of brass, which is usually reckoned equal to $1,430; but if we suppose each pound of brass to contain twenty-four *asses*, as was the case afterwards, it will amount $34,320. This class was subdivided into eighty centuries. To these were added eighteen centuries of *equites;* in all, ninety-eight centuries.

The second class consisted of twenty centuries, whose estates were worth at least seventy-five thousand *asses*. To these were added two centuries of artificers, carpenters, smiths, &c., to manage the engines of war.

The third class was also divided into twenty centuries; their estate was worth fifty thousand *asses*.

The fourth class contained likewise twenty centuries, and their estate was twenty-five thousand *asses*.

The fifth class was divided into thirty centuries; their estate was eleven thousand *asses*.

The sixth class comprehended all those who either had no estates or were not worth so much as those of the fifth class. Their number was greater than that of any of the other classes, yet they were reckoned as but one century.

Thus the whole number of centuries in all the classes was one hundred and ninety-one. By this arrangement the chief power was vested in the richest citizens who composed the first class, which, though least in numbers,

consisted of more centuries than all the rest
taken together; but these likewise bore the
expenditures in peace and war in proportion.

Those of the first class were called *classici;*
all the rest were said to be *infra classem,*
(below the class.)   Hence *classici auctores,*
(classical authors,) for the most approved
authors.

The *comitia centuriata* were held for creating
magistrates, enacting laws, and for trials.
They were assembled by an edict, and were
summoned at least seventeen days before the
time of meeting, that the people might have
time to deliberate on the business to be transacted.

Those who sought any office were called
candidati, from a white robe (*toga candida*)
which they wore.   They were obliged to be
present at the time of the election, and to
declare themselves before the *comitia* were
summoned.   For a long time before the election they endeavored to gain the favor of the
people by every popular art, such as shaking
hands with those they met, visiting them at
their houses, &c.

The auspices were taken on the day of the
comitia, and if they were unfavorable the *comitia* was adjourned for another day.   The *comitia* were also stopped if any person during the
time of the meeting was seized with epilepsy,
or if a tribune of the people interceded with
his *veto,* or if a tempest arose; but in this last

case the election of the magistrates, who were already created, was not rendered invalid.

When there was no obstruction to the *comitia*, on the day appointed the people met in the *Campus Martius*. The magistrates who presided repeated a form of prayer, and then in a speech informed the people what business was to be transacted. If magistrates were to be elected, the names of the candidates were read aloud. If a law was to be passed, it was recited by a herald, and persons were allowed to speak for or against it. A similar form was observed at trials.

The *centuria prærogativa* was that century which obtained by ballot the privilege of voting first. The centuries being called by a herald in their order, went each of them into an enclosure, (*septum* or *ovile*.) In going to this they had to cross over a little bridge where they received from certain officers (called *diribitores*) ballots, on which, if magistrates were to be created, were inscribed the names of the candidates, or rather, their initial letters. Of these tablets, every one threw which he pleased into a chest. When a century had all voted, the votes were counted and another century was called upon to come and vote. If the votes of a century were equal, it was reckoned as nothing, except in trials, in which the century which did not condemn was supposed to acquit.

If a law was to be passed or any thing ordered, ,they received two tablets or ballots; on one were the letters *U. R.*, i. e. *Uti Rogas*, (as you propose;) and on the other *A*, for *Antiquo*, (ancient,) I like the old law, or am opposed to the new law. When a law was passed, it was engraved on brass, and carried to the treasury. It was also fixed up in some public place where it might be easily read.

In the *Comitia Tributa* the people voted, divided into tribes according to their regions or wards. They were held to create the inferior city magistrates, as the ædiles, tribunes of the people, quæstors, &c.; all the magistrates of the provinces, pro-consuls, pro-prætors, &c., the inferior priests; to make laws, (which were called *plebiscita*,) and to hold trials where fines were to be imposed. Capital trials were held only at the *comitia centuriata*. At the *Comitia tributa* the votes of all the citizens were of equal force, and therefore the patricians but seldom attended them.

Section VI.

The Senate.

The Senate (*senatus*) was instituted by Rom ulus to be the perpetual council of the republic. At first it consisted of one hundred members, which were chosen from the Patricians. The senators were called *patres*, (fathers,) either on account of their age, or their paternal care of the state ; and their descendants were called *patricii*. After the Sabines were taken into the city, another hundred was chosen from them by the suffrages of the *curiæ*. Tarquinius Priscus, the fifth king of Rome, added one hundred more, who were called *patres minorum gentium*. Those who had been created by Romulus were called *patres majorum gentium*. In the time of Julius Cæsar the number of senators was increased to nine hundred, and afterwards to one thousand, but Augustus reduced the number to six hundred. Such as were chosen into the senate by Brutus, after the expulsion of Tarquin the Proud, to supply the place of those whom that king had slain, were called *Conscripti*, i. e. persons *written* or *enrolled together with* the old senators who were called *patres*. Hence the expression *Patres Conscripti* which was afterwards applied to all the senators.

Persons were chosen into the senate first by the kings, after their expulsion by the consuls, and by the military tribunes, but from A. U. 310 by the censors ; at first only from the Patricians, but afterwards also from the Plebeians—chiefly, however, from the *Equites*. He whose name was entered first in the censor's books was called *Princeps Senatus*, which title conferred rank only, not power.

The age at which one might be chosen a

senator is not sufficiently ascertained, but was probably not under thirty. The first civil office which gave admission into the senate, was the Quæstorship. He did not, however, thereby become a senator, unless he was chosen into that order by the censors. Sometimes persons procured admission also into the senate by military service. The *Flamen Dialis*, or priest of Jupiter, had a seat in the senate in right of his office, which none of the other priests enjoyed. Regard was had to the fortune of a person before he could become a senator. An estate of four hundred sestertia, and in after times, of twelve hundred, was requisite.

The badges of the senators were,—1. The *Latus Clavus* or *Tunica laticlavia*, which was a tunic with an oblong broad stripe of purple, like a riband, sewed to it, on the fore part. It was broad, to distinguish it from that of the *Equites*, who wore a narrow one.—2. Black buskins reaching to the middle of the leg, with the letter *C*, in silver, on the top of the foot.— 3. A particular place at the public spectacles.

The dictator, consuls, and in their absence the prætors, the military tribunes, the tribunes of the people, and the interrex, had the power of assembling the senate. It was at first assembled by a public officer, called *viator*, but in later times, by an edict. If any senator refused or neglected to attend, he was punished by a fine, and by distraining his goods, unless he had a just excuse. But after the age of sixty, the senators might attend or not, as they pleased.

The senate could not be held except in a temple, that is, in a place consecrated by the augurs ; that thus their deliberations might be rendered more solemn. Anciently, there were but three places where it could meet, two within the city, and the temple of Bellona without it. Afterwards there were several other places where it convened.

On two special occasions the senate was held without the city in the temple of Bellona, or of Apollo, for the reception of foreign ambassadors, and to give audience to their own generals, who were never allowed to come within the city walls while in actual command.

When a report was brought that an ox had spoken, (a thing frequently mentioned in ancient authors,) the senate met in the open air.

The stated meetings of the senate (*senatus legitimus*) were on the kalends, nones, and ides of every month, but after the time of Augustus, on the kalends and ides. An extraordinary meeting (*senatus indictus*, or *edictus*) might be called upon any other day, except the *dies comitialis*, and even then, in dangerous conjunctures, in which case the senate might postpone the *comitia*.

No decree could be made unless there was a quorum. What number constituted a quorum is uncertain. If any one wished to hinder a decree from being passed, and suspected there was not a quorum, he said to the magistrate presiding, " *numera senatum,*" count the senate.

The magistrate who was to hold the senate, offered a sacrifice, and took the auspices before he entered the senate house. If the auspices were unfavorable, or not rightly taken, the business was deferred to another day. Augustus ordered that each senator, before he took his seat, should pay his devotions, with an offering of frankincense and wine, at the altar of that god in whose temple they were to assemble, that thus they might discharge their duty the more religiously.

When the consuls entered the senate house, the senators commonly rose up to do them honor.

The senate was consulted about every thing pertaining to the administration of the state, except the creation of magistrates, the passing of laws, and the determination of war and peace, all which properly belonged to the Roman people.

When a full house was assembled, the presiding magistrate laid the business before them in a set form, and the senators were asked their opinion. The *princeps senatus* was first requested to give his opinion, unless consuls elect were present, who were always asked first. So the prætors, tribunes, &c., elect, seem to have had the same preference before the rest of their order

Nothing could be laid before the senate against the will of the consuls, unless by the tribunes of the people, who might also give their negative against any decree by the solemn word *Veto*, which was called interceding, (*intercedere*.) This might also be done by all who had an equal or greater authority than the magistrate presiding.

The senators delivered their opinion standing; but when they only assented to the opinion of another, they continued sitting.

It was not lawful for the consuls to interrupt those who spoke, although they introduced in their speeches many things foreign to the subject: which they sometimes did, that they might waste the day in speaking ; for no new reference could be made after the tenth hour, i. e. four o'clock in the afternoon, nor a decree passed after sunset, except on very extraordinary occasions.

Those who abused this right of speaking were sometimes forced to yield, by the noise and clamor of the other senators.

In matters of very great importance, the senators sometimes delivered their opinion upon oath. They sometimes made their address to the house by the title of *patres conscripti*, sometimes to the consul, or presiding officer.

When several opinions had been offered and each supported by a number of senators, the presiding magistrate might first put to vote which opinion he pleased, or suppress altogether what he disapproved. And herein consisted the chief power of the consul in the senate. A decree was made by a separation of the senators to different parts of the house. He who presided said, " Let those who are of such an opinion pass over to that side, those who think differently to this." Those senators who only voted but did not speak, or, as some say, who had the right of voting but not of speaking, were called *pedarii*, because they signified their opinion by their feet, not by their tongues. When a decree was made without any opinions being asked or given, it was called *senatus consultum per discessionem*. But when the opinions of the senators were asked, it was simply called *senatus consultum*.

When secrecy was necessary, the clerks and other attendants were not admitted, but what was passed was written out by one of the senators, and the decree was called *tacitum*.

Public registers (*acta*) were kept of what was done in the assemblies of the people, and by courts of justice, also of births, funerals, marriages, divorces, &c.

In writing a decree of the senate, the time and place were put first, then the names of those who were present at the engrossing of it, after that, the motion, with the name of the magistrate who proposed it, to all which was subjoined what the senate decreed.

The decrees of the senate, when written out,

were laid up in the treasury, where also the laws, and other writings pertaining to the republic, were kept. Anciently they were kept by the *Ædiles* in the temple of Ceres. The place where these public records were kept was called *tabularium.* The decrees of the senate concerning Cæsar were inscribed in golden letters on columns of silver. Several decrees still exist, engraven on tables of brass.

The decrees of the senate, when not carried to the treasury, were reckoned invalid. Hence it was ordained under Tiberius, that their decrees, especially concerning the capital punishment of any one, should not be carried to the treasury before the tenth day, that the emperor, if absent from the city, might have an opportunity of considering them, and, if he thought proper, of mitigating them.

Decrees of the senate were rarely reversed. While a question was under debate, every one was at liberty to express his dissent ; but when it was once determined, it was looked upon as the common duty of each member to support the opinion of the majority.

After every thing was finished, the magistrates presiding dismissed the senate with a set form.

The power of the senate was different at different times. Under the regal government, they were mere counsellors of the king, but afterwards every thing was done by their authority   No law could be passed, nor assembly of the people held, without their consent. After the creation of military tribunes, the authority of the senate was in process of time greatly diminished.

Although the supreme power at Rome belonged to the people, yet they seldom enacted any thing without the authority of the senate. In all weighty matters, the method usually observed was, that the senate should first deliberate and decree, and then the people order. But there were many things of great importance which the senate always determined itself, unless when they were brought before the people by the intercessions of the tribunes. This right it seems to have enjoyed not from any express law, but by the custom of their ancestors.

The senate assumed to themselves the guardianship of the public religion ; so that no new god could be introduced, nor altar erected, nor the Sybilline books* consulted without their order.   They had the direction of the treasury; they settled the provinces which were annually assigned to the consuls and prætors ; they nominated out of their own body all ambassadors sent from Rome, and gave to foreign ambassadors what answers they thought proper ; they decreed all public thanksgivings for victories, and conferred the honors of an ovation or triumph, with the title of *imperator*, on their

* See Chap. IV. Sec. II

victorious generals, they could decree the title of king to any prince whom they pleased, and declare any one an enemy by a vote; they inquired into public crimes and treasons within Rome or the other parts of Italy, and heard and determined all disputes among the allied and dependent cities; they exercised a power not only of interpreting the laws, but of absolving men from the obligation of them; they could postpone the assemblies of the people, and prescribe a change of habit to the city in cases of any imminent danger or calamity. But the power of the senate was chiefly conspicuous in civil dissensions or dangerous tumults within the city, in which they passed that solemn decree, " that the consuls should take care that the republic should receive no harm." By this decree, an absolute power was granted to the consuls to punish and put to death whom they pleased, without the form of a trial; to raise forces, and carry on war without the order of the people.

Although the decrees of the senate had not properly the force of laws, and took place mostly in those matters which were not provided for by the laws, yet they were understood always to have a binding force, and were therefore obeyed by all orders. The consuls themselves were obliged to submit to them. In the last ages of the republic the authority of the senate was little regarded by the leading men and their creatures, who by means of bribery obtained from a corrupt populace what they desired, in defiance of the senate.

Section VII.

Courts of Justice, and Judicial Proceedings in Civil and Criminal Trials.

The Judicial Proceedings (*judicia*) of the Romans were either private or public, or in modern terms, *civil* or *criminal*.

The *judicia privata*, or civil trials, were concerning private causes, or differences between private persons. In these at first the kings presided, then the consuls, but after A. U. 379, the prætor. The judicial power of the prætor was called *jurisdictio*, and of the prætors who presided at criminal trials *quæstio*.

On court days, early in the morning, the prætor went to the forum, and there being seated on his tribunal, ordered an *accensus* to call out to the people around that it was the third hour, and whoever had any cause might bring it before him. This could be done only by a certain form.

If a person had a difference with any one, and the matter could not be settled privately, the plaintiff (*actor* or *petitor*) ordered his adversary to go with him before the prætor. If he refused to go, the prosecutor took some one present to witness his refusal, and then the plaintiff might drag the defendant (*reus*) to court by force. It was unlawful to force any one to court from his own house, because a man's house was esteemed his sanctuary. But if any lurked at home to elude a prosecution he was summoned three times, with an interval of ten days between each summons, by the voice of a herald, by letters, or by the edict of the prætor; and if he still did not appear, the prosecutor was put in possession of his effects.

When both parties appeared before the prætor, the plaintiff proposed the action (*actio*) which he intended to bring against the defendant, and demanded from the prætor a writ (*formula*) for that purpose. At the same time the defendant requested that an advocate, or lawyer, should be assigned to him to assist with his counsel. The writ being obtained, the plaintiff offered it to the defendant or dictated to him the words. This writ it was unlawful to change, and the greatest caution was also requisite in drawing it up, for if there was a mistake in one word the whole cause was lost. The plaintiff then required that the defendant should give bail for his appearance in court (*vades dare* or *vadimonium promittere*) on a certain day, which was usually the third day after. When the day came, if either party when cited was not present, he lost his cause unless he had a valid excuse.

F

Actions were either real, personal, or mixed. A real action (*actio in rem*) was for obtaining a thing to which one had a real right, but which was possessed by another. A personal action (*actio in personam*) was against a person to bind him to do or to give something which he was bound to do or give by reason of a contract; or for some wrong done him by the plaintiff. A mixed action had relation both to persons and things.

A sum of money was deposited by both parties in a suit, called *sacramentum*, which fell to the gaining party after the cause was determined; or a stipulation was made about the payment of a certain sum called *sponsio*. Either party lost his cause in real actions, if he refused to enter into this stipulation or to deposite the money required.

Personal actions, called also *condictiones*, were very numerous. In verbal bargains or stipulations there were fixed forms usually observed between the two parties. He who gave a wrong account of a thing to be disposed of was bound to make up the damage. In all important contracts, bonds (*syngraphæ*) formally written out, signed and sealed, were mutually exchanged between the parties.

Actions for a private wrong were of four kinds, for theft, (*ex furto*,) for robbery, (*ex rapina*,) for damage, (*ex damno*,) and for personal injury, (*ex injuria*.)

There were different kinds of judges (*ju-*

dices) or jurymen. A *judex* judged both of fact and law, but only in such cases as were easy and of small importance, and then according to a fixed law or form. An *arbiter* determined what seemed equitable in a thing not sufficiently defined by law. *Recuperatores* judged about recovering and restoring private things, and afterwards in other matters. *Centumviri* were judges chosen from the thirty-five tribes, three from each. They judged chiefly concerning testaments and inheritances.

In the trial, the plaintiff proposed to the defendant such judge or judges as he thought proper. The defendant might object to the judge, and then another was named. The prætor might, if he thought proper, appoint different judges from those chosen by the parties, although he seldom did so; and no one could refuse to act as *judex* when required, without a just cause.

The prætor prescribed the number of witnesses to be called, which commonly did not exceed ten. After this followed a short narration of the cause (*Litis contestatio*) by both parties, corroborated by the testimony of witnesses, and the parties warned each other to attend the third day after.

When this day arrived, the trial proceeded, unless the judge or some of the parties were absent from a necessary cause, in which case the trial was adjourned. If the judge was present, he first took an oath that he would judge according to law, according tc the best of his judgment. The judge generally assumed some lawyers (*consiliarii*) to assist him with their counsel. The judge or judges determined how long each advocate should plead the cause. The pleadings being ended, judgment was given after mid-day, according to the law of the twelve tables. If there was any difficulty in the cause the judge took some time to consider it, and if, after all, he remained uncertain, he said "*nihi non liquet*," "I am not clear." And thus the affair was either left undetermined, or the cause was again returned. If there were several judges, judgment was given according to the opinion of the majority. If their opinions were equal, it was left to the prætor to determine.

After judgment was given and the lawsuit was determined, the conquered party was obliged to do or pay what was decreed, and if he failed or did not find securities (*sponsores*) within thirty days, he was given up by the prætor to his adversary, and led away by him to servitude.

After sentence was passed, the matter could not be altered except where it was discovered that some mistake or fraud had been committed. There was an appeal (*appellatio*) from an inferior to a superior magistrate and court. If after the cause was decided the defendant was acquitted, he might bring an action against the plaintiff for false accusation, (*calumnia.*)

Criminal trials (*publica judicia*) were at first held and judged by the kings and consuls, and then by the people, or by inquisitors (*quæsitors*) appointed by the people. Afterwards certain prætors always took cognizance of certain crimes, and the senate or people seldom interfered except by way of appeal.

Trials before the people (*judicia ad populum*) were, after the institution of the *comitia centuriata* and *tributa*, held in them; capital trials in the *comitia centuriata*; and trials concerning a fine, in the *tributa*. The method of proceeding in both *comitia* was the same; and it was requisite that some magistrate should be the accuser.

The magistrate, who was to accuse any one, having called an assembly and mounted the *Rostra*,* gave notice that he would on a certain day accuse a particular person of a particular crime, and ordered that the person accused (*reus*) should then be present. In the mean time the criminal was kept in custody, unless he found persons to give security for his appearance.

At the day of the trial, any equal or superior magistrate might, by his negative, hinder the trial from proceeding.

---

* *Rostra* properly signified the beaks of ships, and as the tribunal or stage was adorned with these. it was called *rostra.*

The criminal usually stood under the *rostra* in a mean garb, where he was exposed to the scoffs and railleries of the people. The accuser repeated his charge three times, with the intervention of a day between each, and supported it by witnesses and other proofs. An advocate (*patronus*) was permitted to make a defence for the criminal, in which every thing was introduced which could serve to gain the favor of the people, or excite their compassion.

Then the *comitia* were summoned against a certain day, in which the people by their suffrages should determine the fate of the criminal. The criminal having laid aside his usual robe, put on a ragged and old gown, and in this garb went round and supplicated the citizens in his behalf. His friends and relations and others who chose, did the same.

The people gave their votes in the same manner in a trial as in passing a law.

In criminal trials before the prætor, the *judices* were chosen, at different periods of the republic, from the senators and *equites*, sometimes from one order, sometimes from both, and occasionally from the plebeians. The number of the judices were different at different times, varying from three hundred to six hundred.

Of defenders (*defensores*) there were four kinds ; *patroni*, who pleaded the cause ; *advocati*, who assisted by their counsel; *procuratores*, attorneys who managed the business of a person in his absence; and *cognitores*, who defended the cause of a person when present. The two latter were employed only in private trials.

The proofs were of three kinds; the declaration of slaves extorted by torture, (*quæstiones ;*) the testimony of free citizens, (*testes ;*) and writings, (*tabulæ.*)

A false witness was thrown from the Tarpeian rock; except in war, when he was beaten to death with sticks by his fellow-soldiers.

The prætor gave to each *judex* three tables; on one was written the letter *C.,* for *condemno,* 'I condemn;' on another the letter *A.,* for *absolvo,* 'I acquit;' or on the third, *N. L., non liquet,* 'I cannot decide.' Each of the *judices* threw which of these tablets he thought proper into an urn. The prætor having taken these out and counted them, pronounced sentence according to the opinion of the majority. If the number of judges who condemned, and of those who acquitted was equal, the criminal was acquitted.

While the *judices* were putting the ballots into the urn, the criminal and his friends threw themselves at their feet, and employed every method to excite their compassion.

The prætor, when about to pronounce a sentence of condemnation, laid aside his *toga prætexta.*

Section VIII.

Punishments.

Punishments among the Romans were of eight kinds.

1. *Mulcta* or *damnum*, a fine, which at first never exceeded two oxen and thirty sheep, or the valuation of them.

2. *Vincula*, bonds, which included public and private custody; *public*, in prison, (*carcer;*) and *private*, when delivered to magistrates to be kept at their houses (*in libera custodia*) till they should be tried. Under the name of *vincula*, were comprehended *catenæ*, chains; *compedes*, or *pedicæ*, or fetters for the feet; *manicæ*, manacles or bonds for the hands; *nervus*, an iron shackle for the feet or neck; a wooden frame with holes, called also *columbar;* and *boiæ*, leathern thongs and iron chains, for tying the neck or feet.

3. *Verbera*, beating or scourging with sticks or staves, (*fustes;*) with rods, (*virgæ;*) with whips or lashes, (*flagella.*)

4. *Talio*, retaliation, a punishment similar to the injury, as an eye for an eye, a limb for a limb, &c. This punishment seems to have been very rarely inflicted.

5. *Ignominia* or *infamia*, disgrace or infamy, inflicted by the censors, by the law, or by the edict of the prætor. Those made *infamous* by

a judicial sentence, were deprived of their dignity, and rendered ineligible to public offices; sometimes also incapable of being wit-nesses or of making a will; hence called *intestabiles*.

6. *Exilium*, banishment or exile. This word was not used in a judicial sentence, but *aquæ et ignis interdictio*, 'forbidding one the use of fire and water,' whereby a person was banished from Italy, but might go to any other place he might wish. Augustus introduced two new forms of banishment, *deportatio*,* perpetual banishment ; *relegatio*, either a temporary or perpetual banishment without a deprivation of rights and fortunes.

7. *Servitus*, slavery. Those were sold as slaves who did not give in their names to be enrolled in the censor's books, or refused to enlist as soldiers ; because they were thus supposed to have voluntarily renounced the rights of citizens.

8. *Mors*, death. Banishment and slavery were called a *civil* death. Only the most heinous crimes were punished by a violent death. In ancient times it appears to have been the most usual practice to hang malefactors, afterwards to scourge and behead them, (*securi percutere ;*) to throw them from the Tarpeian rock, (*de saxo Tarpeio dejicere ;*) or from that

---

* In this form of banishment, the condemned were deprived of their rights and fortunes, and banished to a certain place, without permission to go anywhere else.

part of the prison called *Robur;* and to stran-
gle them in prison.

The bodies of criminals were not burned or
buried; but exposed before the prison, usually
on certain stairs called *gemoniæ*, and then
dragged with a hook, and thrown into the Tiber. Sometimes, however, their friends purchased the right of burying them.

Under the Emperors several new and more
severe punishments were contrived; as expos-
ing to wild beasts, burning alive, &c. When
criminals were burnt, they were dressed in a
tunic spread over with pitch and other combustible matter.

, Sometimes persons were condemned to the
public works, to engage with wild beasts, or
fight as gladiators, or were employed as public slaves in attending on the public baths, in
cleansing common sewers, or repairing the
streets and highways.

Slaves, after being scourged, were crucified,
usually with a label or inscription on their
breast intimating their crime. In the time of
Augustus a new species of cruelty to slaves
was devised—that of throwing them into a
fish-pond to be devoured by lampreys, (*mu-
rænæ.*)

A person guilty of parricide, that is, of mur-
dering a parent or any near relation, after
having been severely scourged, was sewed up
in a sack (*culeus*) with a dog, a cock, a viper,
and an ape, and then thrown into the sea.

Section IX.

Public and Private Rights of Roman Citizens and of Foreigners.

While Rome was but small and thinly inhabited, whoever fixed their abode in the city, or Roman territory, obtained the rights of citizens.

Besides those who had settled in the Roman territory, the freedom of the city was afterwards granted to several foreign towns, which were then called *municipia* and the inhabitants *municipes*, and some of these might enjoy offices at Rome.

But when the Roman empire was more widely extended, and the dignity of a Roman citizen began to be more valued, the freedom of the city (*jus civitatis*) was more sparingly conferred, and in different degrees, according to the merits of the allies towards the republic.

The rights of Roman citizens were either public or private ; the former were called *jus civitatis*, and the latter, *jus Quiritium.*

The public rights of Roman citizens were—

1. *Jus census,* the right of being enrolled in the censor's books.

2. *Jus militiæ,* the right of serving in the army, which at first was peculiar to the higher order of citizens, but afterwards, under the emperors, soldiers were taken not only from

Italy and the provinces, but also from barbarous nations.

3. *Jus tributorum*, the right of taxation, which was publicly imposed upon each individual through the tribes, in proportion to the valuation of his estates.

4. *Jus suffragii*, the right of voting in the different assemblies of the people.

5. *Jus honorum*, the right of bearing public offices in the state, which were either priesthoods or magistracies, and at first were conferred only on Patricians, but afterwards were nearly all shared with the Plebeians.

6. *Jus sacrorum*, the right of religious solemnities, which were either public, those performed at the public expense ; or private, those which every one privately observed at home. Every father of a family had his household gods which he worshipped at home.

It was a maxim among the Romans that no one could be a citizen of Rome who suffered himself to be made a citizen of any other city. If any foreigner who had obtained the freedom of Rome returned to his native city and became a citizen of it, he ceased to be a Roman citizen.

The *jus Latii* was the rights which the inhabitants of Latinum enjoyed, and which were but little inferior to the *jus civitatis* of the city.

The *jus Italicum* was a right enjoyed by the inhabitants of *Italia*, inferior to the *jus Latii*.

All those who were not citizens, were called foreigners, (*peregrini*,) but afterwards the inhabitants of the whole world were divided into Romans and Barbarians. Foreigners might live in the city, but they enjoyed none of the privileges of citizens. They were subject to a particular jurisdiction, and sometimes were expelled from the city at the pleasure of the magistrates. They could not wear the Roman dress, nor had they the right of legal property, or of making a will. When a foreigner died, his goods were either reduced into the treasury as having no heir, or if he had attached himself to any person as a patron, that person succeeded to his effects. But in process of time the inconveniences were removed, and foreigners were elevated to the highest honors in the state.

The private rights of Roman citizens were, 1. *Jus Libertatis*, the right of liberty;—2. *Jus Gentilitatis et Familiæ*, the right of family;— 3. *Jus Connubii*, the right of marriage;—4. *Jus Patrium*, the right of a father;—5. *Jus Dominii Legitimi*, the right of legal property; —6. *Jus Testamenti et Hereditatis*, the right of making a will, and of succeeding to an inheritance ;—7. *Jus Tutelæ*, the right of tutelage or wardship.

1. The right of liberty comprehended *freedom* not only from the power of masters, but also from the dominion of tyrants, the severity of magistrates, the cruelty of creditors, and

the insolence of more powerful citizens. After the expulsion of Tarquin, a law was made, that no one should be king at Rome, and that whoever should form a design of making himself king, might be slain with impunity. At the same time the people were bound by an oath, that they would never suffer a king to be created.

Roman citizens were secured against the tyrannical treatment of magistrates, by the right of appealing from them to the people, and that the person who appealed, should in no manner be punished till the people determined the matter; but chiefly by the assistance of the tribunes.

None but the whole Roman people in the *comitia centuriata*, could pass sentence on the life of a Roman citizen. The simple expression, "I am a Roman citizen," checked their severest decrees.

By the laws of the twelve tables, it was ordained that insolvent debtors should be given up to their creditors to be bound in fetters and cords, whence they were called *nexi, obærati,* and *addicti.* And although they did not entirely lose the rights of freemen, yet they were nevertheless in actual slavery, and frequently treated more harshly than even slaves themselves.

To check the cruelty of usurers, a law was made A. U. 429, that no debtors should be kept in irons or bonds; that the goods of the debtor, not his person, should be given up to his creditors.

2. The right of family. Each *gens*, and each family, had certain sacred rights peculiar to itself, which went by inheritance in the same manner as effects. When heirs by the father's side of the same family became extinct, those of the same *gens* succeeded in preference to relations by the mother's side of the same family. No one could pass from a Patrician family to a Plebeian, or from a Plebeian to a Patrician, except by a form of adoption, which could only be made at the *comitia curiata*.

3. The right of marriage. No Roman citizen was permitted to marry a slave, a barbarian, or a foreigner, unless by the permission of the people. By the laws of the *Decemviri*, intermarriages between the Patricians and Plebeians were prohibited. But this restriction was soon abolished. But when a Patrician lady married a Plebeian, she was excluded from the sacred rights of Patrician ladies.

4. The right of a father. A father among the Romans had the power of life and death over his children. He could not only expose them when infants, but even when grown up he might imprison, scourge, send them bound to work in the country, and also put them to death by any punishment he pleased.

A son could acquire no property but with

his father's consent, and what he did thus acquire, was called his *peculium*, as that of a slave.

The power of the father was suspended when the son was promoted to any public office, but not extinguished ; for it continued not only during the life of the children, but likewise extended to grandchildren and great-grandchildren. None of them became entirely their own masters (*sui juris*) till the death of their father and grandfather. A daughter, by marriage, passed from the power of her father under that of her husband.

A father could render a son free from his authority, by a form of emancipation similar to that used in giving a slave his freedom, except in the case of the slave he was sold but once, while a son was sold three times before the prætor.

When a man had no children of his own, lest his sacred rights and name should be lost, he might assume strangers (*extranei*) as his children by adoption.

5. The right of property. Things with respect to property among the Romans were variously divided. Some things were said to be of divine right, and were held sacred, (*res sacra*,) as altars, temples, or any thing publicly consecrated to the gods by the authority of the pontiffs ; or religious, (*religiosæ*,) as sepulchres; or inviolable, (*sanctæ*,) as the walls and gates of a city. Other things were said to be of

human right, and were called profane, (*pro-fanæ*.) These were either public and common, as the air, running water, the sea, &c.; or private, which might be the property of individuals.   Private things were either *res mancipi*, those which might be sold, or the possession of them transferred from one person to another; and *nec mancipi res*, those things which could not be thus transferred.

The transferring of property was made by a certain act called *mancipatio*, in which the same formalities were observed as in emancipating a son, only that it was done but once.

There were other modes of acquiring legal property, as *jure cessio*, when a person gave up his effects to any one before the prætor, who adjudged them to the person who claimed them, as in the case of debtors giving up their goods to their creditors; *usucaptio*, when one obtained the property of a thing by possessing it for a certain time without interruption, (*usurpatio ;*) *emitio sub corona*, purchasing captives in war; *auctio*, when things were exposed to public sale; *adjudicatio*, which took place in dividing an inheritance among co-heirs, in dividing a joint stock among partners, and in settling boundaries among neighbors; *donatio*, donation, gift, or dowry.

6. The right of testament and inheritance. None but Roman citizens could make a will or be witness to it, or inherit any thing by it.

The usual method of making a will was by

G

money and scales, (*per æs et libram*,) where in the presence of five witnesses, a weigher, (*libripens*,) and his witness, (*antestatus*,) the testator, by an imaginary sale, disposed of his family and property to one who was called *familiæ emptor*, who was not the heir, but was only admitted for the sake of form, that it might appear that the testator had alienated his effects in his lifetime. This act was called *familiæ mancipatio*. These formalities were not always observed, especially in later times. It was considered sufficient if one subscribed his will, or even named his heir *viva voce* before seven witnesses.

Testaments were subscribed by the testator, and usually by the witnesses, and sealed with their seals or rings. They were likewise tied with a thread drawn thrice through holes, and sealed. Like all other civil deeds, they were always written in Latin. (A legacy expressed in Greek was not valid.) These were deposited either privately in the hands of a friend, or in a temple with the keeper of it.

When additions were made to a will they were called *codicilli*. If any one died without making a will (*intestatus*) his property descended to his nearest relations, first to his children ; or failing them, to his nearest relations by the father's side ; and failing them, to those of the same *gens*.

7. The right of tutelage or wardship. A father might leave whom he pleased as guar-

dians (*tutores*) to his children. But if he died intestate, this charge devolved by law on the nearest relation by the father's side. This gave occasion to many frauds, to the injury of wards, (*pupilli*.)

When there was no guardian by testament, nor a legal one, then a guardian was appointed to minors and to women, by the prætor and the majority of the tribunes of the people.

Women could not transact any business of importance without the concurrence of their parents, husbands, or guardians; and a husband at his death might appoint a guardian to his wife, or leave her the choice of her own guardians.

SECTION X.

Revenues and Administration of Finance.

There were several sources of revenue among the Romans. *Tributum* was a tax publicly imposed on the people, which was exacted from each individual through the tribes, in proportion to the valuation of his estates. Money publicly exacted on any other account, was called *vectigal*.

There were three kinds of tribute: one imposed equally on each person; another according to valuation of his property; and a third which was extraordinary, and demanded only in cases of necessity. This last was, in many cases, voluntary ; and an account of it was taken that when the treasury was again enriched it might be repaid, as was done after the second Punic war.

After the expulsion of the kings, the poor were for some time exempted from the burden of taxes until the year A. U. 349, when the senate decreed that pay should be given from the treasury to the common soldiers in the army who had hitherto served at their own ex pense ; whereupon all were obliged to con- tribute annually, according to their fortune, for the pay of the soldiers. In the year of the city 586, annual tributes were remitted on ac- count of the immense sums brought into the treasury by L. Paulus Æmilius after the defeat of Perseus ; and this immunity from taxes continued down to the time of Julius Cæsar.

The other taxes (*vectigalia*) were of three kinds, *portorium, decumæ,* and *scriptura.*

1. *Portorium* was money paid at the port for goods imported and exported, the collectors of which were called *portitores ;* or for carrying goods over a bridge, where every carriage paid a certain sum to the exactor of the toll.

2. *Decumæ,* tithes, were the tenth part of corn, and the fifth part of other fruits, which were exacted from those who tilled the public lands, either in Italy or without it. Those who farmed the tithes were called *decumani,*

and esteemed the most honorable of the publicans, as agriculture was esteemed the most honorable way of making a fortune among the Romans.

3. *Scriptura* was the tax paid from public pastures and woods, so called because those who wished to feed their cattle there *subscribed* their names before the farmer of them, and paid a certain sum for each beast.

All these taxes were let, publicly, by the censors at Rome. Those who farmed them were called *publicani* or *mancipes*. They also gave security (*prædes*) to the people, and had partners who shared the profit and loss with them.

There was, for a long time, a tax upon salt; and another called *vicesima*, which was the twentieth part of the value of any slave who was freed. Various other taxes were imposed by the emperors, as the hundredth part of things to be sold, the twentieth of inheritances, taxes on eatables, &c. The people of the provinces, besides the *scripturæ*, were obliged to furnish a certain number of cattle from their flock. They also paid a tax for journeys, especially for carrying a corpse, which could not be transported from one place to another without the permission of the high priest, or of the emperor. But this tax was afterwards abolished.

There was a tax on iron, silver, and gold mines, on marble, and on salt-pits.

The *quæstors* were the treasurers of the republic. Two of these remained at Rome, and were called *quæstores urbani :* the rest, *provinciales* or *militares.* The principal charge of the city quæstors was the care of the treasury, which was kept in the temple of Saturn. They received and expended the public money, exacted the fines imposed by the people, &c. The money thus raised was called *argentum multatitium.*

CHAPTER III.

MILITARY AND NAVAL AFFAIRS OF THE ROMANS.

SECTION I.

Manner of Declaring War and Levying Soldiers.

THE Romans were a nation of warriors. During the existence of their republic they were almost always engaged in wars; first, with the different states of Italy for five hundred years, and then for about two hundred years more, in subduing the various countries which composed that immense empire.

The Romans never engaged in any war

without solemnly proclaiming it. This was done by a set of priests called *feciales*.

When the Romans thought themselves injured by any nation, they sent one or more of these *feciales* to demand redress ; and if it was not immediately given, thirty-three days were granted to consider the matter, after which war might be lawfully declared. Then the *feciales* again went to their confines, and having thrown a bloody spear into them, formally declared war against that nation. Afterwards, when the empire was enlarged and wars were carried on with distant nations, this ceremony was performed in a certain field near the city, called *ager hostilis.*

Every citizen was obliged to enlist as a soldier, when the public service required, from the age of seventeen to forty-six ; nor at first, could any one enjoy any office in the city, who had not served ten campaigns. Every foot-soldier was obliged to serve twenty campaigns, and every horseman, ten. At first, none of the lowest class were enlisted as soldiers, nor freedmen, unless in dangerous conjunctures. But this was afterwards altered.

In the first ages of the republic four legions were annually raised, two to each consul ; but afterwards a greater number was raised, even up to thirty legions.

The consuls, after they entered upon their office, appointed a day on which all those who were of the military age should be present in

the capitol, when they cited out of each tribe
such as they pleased, and every one was
obliged to answer to his name under a severe
penalty. Their names were written down on
tables ; hence *scribere*, to enlist, to levy.

In certain wars, and under certain commanders, there was the greatest alacrity to
enlist ; but this was not always the case, and
compulsion, fines, corporal punishment, imprisonment, were then resorted to by the magistrates.

In sudden and dangerous emergencies, as
there was not time to go through the usual
forms, the consul said, " Let every one, who
wishes to save the republic, follow me."   This
was called *conjuratio*.

The cavalry were chosen from the body of
the *Equites*.

After the levy was completed, one soldier
was chosen to repeat over the words of the
military oath, (*sacramentum*,) and the rest swore
after him.   Without this oath no one could
fight against the enemy.

The provinces were required to furnish their
share of infantry and cavalry, called allies,
(*socii*.)   The troops sent by foreign kings and
states were called auxiliaries, (*auxiliares*.)
Under the emperors, the Roman armies were,
in a great measure, composed of foreigners.

Section II.

Division of Troops, their Arms, Armor, Officers and Dress.

After the levy was completed, and the mili
tary oath administered, the troops were form
ed into legions, (*legiones.*)   The number of
men in a legion was different at different
times.   In the time of Polybius, it was 4,200.

Each legion was divided into ten cohorts,
(*cohortes,*) each cohort into three bands, (*maniples,*) and each *maniple* into two centuries ; so
there were in a legion thirty maniples and sixty centuries.   There were usually three hundred cavalry added to each legion, called *jus-
tus equitatus* or *ala.*   They were divided into
ten *turmæ,* or troops, and each *turma* into three
decuriæ, or bodies of ten men.

The different kinds of infantry which composed the legion were three, the *hastati, principes,* and *triarii.*

The *hastati* were so called because they
fought with long spears.   They consisted of
young men in the flower of life, and formed
the first line in battle.

The *principes* were men of middle age in
the vigor of life, who occupied the second line.

The *triarii* were old soldiers of approved
valor, who formed the third line.   They were
H

also called *pilani,* from the *pilum* or javelin which they used.

There was a fourth kind of troops, called *velites,* from their swiftness and agility, who were light-armed soldiers.

These did not form a part of the legion, and had no certain part assigned them, but fought in scattered parties, where occasion required. To them were joined the slingers (*funditores*) and archers, (*sagittarii.*) The *velites* were equipped with bows, slings, seven javelins or spears, a sword, a round buckler, (*parma,*) and a helmet, (*galea.*)

The arms of the *hastati, principes,* and *triarii,* both defensive (*arma ad tegendum*) and offensive, (*tela ad petendum,*) were in a great measure the same. The *scutum* was an oblong shield with an iron boss (*umbo*) four feet long and two and a half broad; the whole covered with a bull's hide. The *clypeus* was a round shield of smaller size.

The *galea* was a helmet of brass or iron, coming down to the shoulders, but leaving the face uncovered. Upon the top of the helmet was the crest, (*crista,*) adorned with plumes of feathers of various colors.

The *lorica* was a coat of mail, generally made of leather covered with plates of iron in the form of scales. *Ocreæ* were greaves for the legs. *Caliga* was a kind of shoe or covering for the feet, set with nails, used chiefly by the common soldiers.

The *gladus* or *ensis* was a sword; the *pilum*, a javelin.

The cavalry at first used their ordinary clothing for the sake of agility, that they might more easily mount their horses; for they used no stirrups, (*stapia*,) as they were afterwards called. Their saddles were only coverings of cloth to sit on, called *ephippia*. But the Roman cavalry afterwards imitated the manner of the Greeks, and used nearly the same armor as the infantry.

In each legion there were six military tribunes who commanded under the consul, each in his turn, generally a month at a time. In battle, a tribune seems to have had the charge of ten centuries.

The tribunes chose the officers who commanded the centuries, called centurions, (*centuriones*,) from the common soldiers, according to their merit. But this office was sometimes disposed of by the consul, or pro-consul. The badge of a centurion was a vine-rod or sapling, (*vitis*.)

The centurions of the first century of the first maniple of the *triarii*, was called *centurio primi pili*, and presided over all the other centurions, and had charge of the eagle (*aquila*) or chief standard of the legion.

Each of the centurions chose two assistants or lieutenants, (*optiones*,) and two standard-bearers or ensigns, (*signiferi*.)

He who commanded the cavalry of a legion

was called *præfectus alæ.* Each *turma* had three *decuriones*, or commanders of ten.

The troops of the allies, which were also called *alæ* from their being stationed on the wings, had præfects (*præfecti*) appointed over them, who commanded in the same manner as the legionary tribunes.

A third part of the horse, and a fifth part of the foot of the allies, were selected and posted near the consul, under the name of *extra-ordinarii*, and one troop called *ablecti*, to serve as his life-guards.

Two legions with the due number of cavalry, and the allies, formed what was called a consular army, (*exercitus consularis*,) about 20,000 men.

The consul appointed lieutenant-generals (*legati*) under him.

The military robe or cloak of the general (*dux*) was called *paludamentum* or *chlamys*, of a scarlet color, bordered with purple. The military cloak of the officers and soldiers was called *sagum*, also *chlamys*.

Section III.

Discipline, Marches, and Encampments.

The discipline of the Roman army was chiefly conspicuous in their marches and encampments. They never passed a night, even in the longest marches, without pitching a camp and fortifying it with a rampart and ditch. Persons were always sent before to choose and mark out a proper place for that purpose, called *metatores*.

When the army stayed but one night in the same camp, it was simply called a camp, (*castra ;*) if it remained a considerable time, it was called a standing-camp, (*castra stativa.*)

The form of the camp was generally square. It was surrounded with a ditch (*fossa*) usually nine feet deep and twelve feet broad; and a rampart (*vellum*) composed of the earth dug from the ditch, and sharp stakes driven into it. The camp had four gates, one on each side, and was divided into two parts, the upper and lower. The upper part was that next to the principal gate, in which was the general's tent, (*prætorium,*) with a sufficient space around for his retinue. On one side of the *prætorium* were the tents of the *legati*, and on the other side that of the *quæstor.* Near this was the *forum*, where things were sold. In this part of the camp were also the tents of the tribunes, prefects, &c.

The lower part of the camp was separate from the upper by a broad open space which extended the whole breadth of the camp, called *principia*.

In this lower part, the troops were disposed in a regular order which never varied; hence all knew their place after the general's tent was once fixed.

The tents (*tentoria*) were covered with leather extended with ropes. In each tent were usually ten soldiers with their *decanus* who commanded them.

In pitching the camp, different divisions of the army were appointed to execute different parts of the work, under the inspection of the tribunes or centurions, as they were likewise during the encampment, to procure water, forage, wood, &c.

A certain number of maniples were appointed to keep guard at the gates, on the rampart, and in other places of the camp, before the *prætorium*, and tents of the principal officers, by day and night, who were changed every three hours. *Excubiæ* denotes watches either by day or night, *vigiliæ* only by night. Guards placed before the gates were properly called *stationes*, on the rampart *custodiæ*. Whoever deserted his post was punished with death. The watchword (*symbolum*) was varied every night by the general.

The signal was given for changing the watches with a trumpet (*tuba*) or horn, (*buccina.*) The other instruments of music in the army were the *cornu*, a horn bent almost round ; and *lituus*, the clarion.

A principal part of the discipline of the camp consisted in exercises, walking, running, leaping, swimming, shooting the arrow, throwing the javelin, attacking the wooden figure of a man as if a real enemy, &c.

When the general thought proper to decamp, every thing was done in its regular order, so that, all knowing their respective duties, no confusion arose from the size and numbers of the army.

An army in close array was called *agmen pilatum.* The form of an army on march varied according to circumstances and the nature of the ground. The soldiers were trained with great care to observe the military pace, (*gradus militaris.*) They usually marched at the rate of twenty miles in five hours, but sometimes faster.

The load which a Roman soldier carried is almost incredible ;—victuals for fifteen or more days, a saw, a basket, a mattock, an axe, a hook, a leathern thong, a chain, a pot, &c., stakes usually three or four, the whole amounting to sixty pounds weight, besides arms. Under this load they marched twenty miles a day, sometimes more.

There were beasts of burden for carrying the tents, mills, baggage, &c.

Order of Battle, Standards, Signals, Sieges, &c.

The Roman army was usually drawn up in three lines, each several rows deep—the *hastati*, in the first line; the *principes*, in the second; and the *triarii*, in the third; at proper distances from one another.

A maniple of each kind of troops was placed behind one another; so that each legion had ten maniples in front. There were intervals or spaces (*viæ*) between the lines and maniples. The *velites* were placed in these spaces, or on the wings.

The Roman legions were placed in the centre, the allies and auxiliaries on the right and left wings, (*cornua.*) The cavalry were sometimes placed behind the infantry, but most commonly on the wings.

This arrangement was not always observed. Sometimes all the different kinds of troops were placed in the same line.

When there were two legions, one legion and its allies were sometimes placed in the first line, and the other behind as a body of reserve. This was called *acies duplex*, and when there was only one line, *acies simplex*. In the time of Cæsar the bravest troops were commonly placed in front, contrary to the ancient custom.

Each century, or at least each maniple, had its proper standard (*signum*, and standard-bearer, (*signifer.*) The ensign of a maniple was anciently a bundle of hay on the top of a pole, afterwards a spear with a cross-piece of wood on the top, sometimes the figure of a hand above; and below, a small round shield of silver, sometimes of gold, on which were represented the images of the warlike deities. Hence the standards were called the deities of the legions, (*numina legionum*,) and worshipped with religious adoration. The soldiers swore by them.

The standards of the different divisions had certain letters inscribed on them, to distinguish the one from the other.

The standard of the cavalry was called *vexillum*, a flag, or banner, which was a square piece of cloth fixed on the end of a spear.

To lose the standard was always esteemed disgraceful, particularly to the standard-bearer: sometimes a capital crime. ᐧHence to animate the soldiers the standards were sometimes thrown amongst the enemy.

A silver eagle with expanded wings on the top of a spear, sometimes holding a thunderbolt in its claws, with the figure of a small chapel above it, was the common standard of the legion.

The general was usually attended by a select band, (*cohors prætoria.*)

When the general, after having consulted

the auspices, had determined to lead forth his troops against the enemy, a red flag was displayed on a spear, from the top of the general's tent, (*pretorium.*)   Then having called an assembly by the sound of a trumpet, he harangued the soldiers, who signified their approbation by shouts, by raising their right hands, or by beating on their shields with their spears. After the harangue the trumpet sounded, which was the signal for marching.   At the same time the soldiers called out "to arms," (*ad arma.*)   The standards, which stood fixed in the ground, were pulled up, and if this were done easily it was reckoned a good omen ; if not, the contrary.   The watchword (*symbolum*) was given, and in the mean time many of the soldiers made their wills.

When the army approached near the enemy, the general, riding round the ranks, again exhorted them to courage, and then gave the signal to engage, upon which all the trumpets sounded and the soldiers rushed forward to the charge with a great shout to animate one another, and intimidate the enemy.

The *velites* first began the battle, and when repulsed, retreated either through the intervals between the files (*ordines*) or by the flanks of the army, and rallied in the rear.   Then the *hastati* advanced, and if they were defeated they retired slowly into the intervals of the ranks of the *principes*, who then engaged; and if they too were defeated, the *triarii* rose up,

(for hitherto they continued in a sitting posture.) Thus the enemy had several fresh attacks to sustain. If the *triarii* were defeated,
the day was lost, and a retreat was sounded
This was the usual manner of attack, but it
often varied.

When the Romans gained a victory, the
soldiers with shouts of joy saluted their general by the title of *imperator*. His lictors
wreathed their *fasces* with laurel, as did also
the soldiers their spears and javelins. He im
mediately sent letters wrapped round with
laurel to the senate to inform them of his success, and if the victory was considerable, to
demand a triumph. If the senate approved
they decreed a thanksgiving to the gods, and
confirmed to the general the title of *imperator*,
which he retained till his triumph, or return
to the city.

The Romans attacked cities and towns
either by a sudden assault, or, if that failed,
they tried to reduce them by a blockade.
They first surrounded the town with troops,
and by their missive-weapons endeavored to
clear the walls of defendants. Then joining
their shields in the form of a tortoise, (*testudo*,)
to secure themselves from the darts of the
enemy, they came up to the gates and tried
either to undermine the walls or scale them.

When a place could not be taken by storm
it was besieged. Two lines of fortification or
intrenchments were drawn around the place,

at some distance from one another, called the lines of contravallation and circumvallation, the one against the sallies of the townsmen, and the other against attacks from without. These lines were composed of a ditch and rampart, strengthened with a parapet and battlements, and sometimes a solid wall of considerable height and thickness, flanked with towers and forts at proper distances, round the whole.

Between the lines were disposed the army of the besiegers. The camp was pitched in a convenient situation to communicate with the lines.

From the inner line was raised a mount (*agger*) composed of earth, wood, hurdles, (*crates*,) and stone, which was gradually advanced towards the town, always increasing in height, till it equalled or overtopped the walls. It was secured by towers consisting of different stories, from which showers of darts and stones were discharged on the townsmen, by means of engines (*tormenta*) called *catapultæ, balistæ,* and *scorpiones,* to defend the work and workmen. The labor and industry of the Roman troops were as remarkable as their courage.

There were also moveable towers which were pushed forward and brought back on wheels fixed below on the inside of the planks. To prevent them from being set on fire by the enemy, they were covered with new hides

and pieces of coarse cloth.   They were of immense bulk, and when they could be brought
up to the walls a place was seldom long able
to resist.

But the most dreadful machine of all was
the battering ram, (*aries ;*) a long beam, like
the mast of a ship, and armed at one end with
iron in the form of a ram's head, whence its
name.   It was covered with sheds, (*vineæ.*)
Under them the besiegers either worked the
ram, or tried to undermine the walls. The
battering ram was suspended by chains fastened to a beam which lay across two posts, and
thus equally balanced, it was violently thrust
forward, drawn back, and again pushed forward, until by repeated blows it had broken
down the wall.   The effects of this machine
were prodigious.   Care was taken to wrap
the beam with wet leather, to prevent its being
set on fire by the enemy.

In the mean time the besieged, to frustrate
the attempts of the besiegers, met their under-
miners, with counterminers, which sometimes
occasioned dreadful conflicts below ground.
When they apprehended that a breach would
be made in the wall, they erected new walls
behind them. They employed various methods
to destroy or weaken the force of the ram,
and to defend themselves from the engines
and darts of the besiegers.

When the Romans besieged a town, and
thought themselves sure of taking it, they used

solemnly to call out of it the gods under whose special protection the place was supposed to be.

When a city was solemnly destroyed, a plough was drawn along where the walls had stood

---

SECTION V.

Military Rewards, Triumphs, Punishments, and Pay.

After a victory, the general assembled his troops, and in the presence of the whole army bestowed rewards on those who had merited them. The highest reward was the civic crown, (*corona civica,*) given to him who had saved the life of a citizen, made of oak leaves. It was attended with particular honors. The person who received it wore it in the public shows, and sat next to the senate.

To persons who first mounted the rampart, or entered the camp of the enemy, was given by the general a castral crown (*corona castrensis*) of gold. To him who first scaled the walls of a city for an assault, was given the mural crown, (*corona muralis ;*) and to him who first boarded the ship of an enemy, a naval crown, (*corona navalis.*)

When an army was freed from a blockade, the soldiers gave to their deliverer a crown made of the grass which grew in the place where they had been blocked up. This crown, called *graminea corona obsidionalis*, was esteemed the greatest of all military honors except a triumph.

Golden crowns were also given to officers and soldiers who had displayed singular bravery.

There were many smaller rewards of various kinds, such as flags of various colors, trappings for horses, ornaments for men, golden chains for the neck, bracelets, &c. These were conferred by the general in the presence of the whole army. They were kept with great care, and worn on public occasions.

The spoils (*spolia*) taken from the enemy were fixed on their door-posts, or in the more conspicuous part of their houses. When the general of the Romans slew the opposing general, the spoils which he took (*spolia opima*) were hung up in the temple of Jupiter Feretrius.

Sometimes soldiers, on account of their bravery, received a double share of corn; also double pay.

The highest military honor which could be obtained in the Roman state, was a triumph, (*triumphus*,) or solemn procession, in which a victorious general and his army passed through the city to the Capitol.

A triumph was decreed by the senate, and sometimes by the people contrary to the will.

of the senate, to the general, who in a just
war against foreigners, and in a single battle,
had slain above five thousand enemies of the
republic, and by that victory had enlarged the
limits of the empire.

As no person could enter the city while invested with military command, generals, on
the day of their triumph, were free from that
restriction.

The triumphal procession began from the
Campus Martius, and went thence along to
the city, and through the most public places of
the city, to the Capitol. The streets were
strewed with flowers, and the altars smoked
with incense. A triumphal arch of sculptured
masonry was erected, under which the procession marched.

First, went musicians of various kinds, singing and playing triumphal songs; next were
led the oxen to be sacrificed, having their
horns gilded, and their heads adorned with
fillets and garlands; then in carriages were
brought the spoils taken from the enemy.
The titles of the conquered nations were inscribed on wooden frames. The captive leaders followed in chains, with their children and
attendants; after them came the lictors, having their *fasces* wreathed with laurel; followed by a great company of musicians and
dancers dressed like Satyrs, and wearing
crowns of gold, in the midst of whom was a
pantomime, clothed in a female garb, whose

business it was, by his looks and gestures, to insult the vanquished. Next followed a long train of persons carrying perfumes. Then came the general, (*dux,*) dressed in purple embroidered with gold, with a crown of laurel on his head, a branch of laurel in his right hand, and in his left a finely-wrought ivory sceptre with an eagle on the top ; having his face painted with vermilion, and a golden ball hanging from his neck, containing some amulet in it, or magical preservative against envy ; standing in a gilded chariot adorned with ivory, and drawn by four white horses, sometimes by elephants ; attended by his relations and a great crowd of citizens, all dressed in white.   And that he might not be too much elated, a slave, carrying a golden crown, sparkling with gems, stood behind him and frequently whispered in his ear, "REMEMBER THAT THOU ART A MAN." After the general, followed the consuls and senators on foot. His *legati* and military tribunes rode by his side.

The victorious army, infantry and cavalry, came last, all in their order crowned with laurel, singing their own and their general's praises, but sometimes throwing out railleries against him ; and often exclaiming " IO TRIUMPHE," in which all the citizens as they passed along joined.

The general, when he began to turn his chariot from the forum to the capitol, usually ordered the captive kings and leaders of the enemy, to be led to prison, and slain; and when he reached the capitol, he waited till he heard that these savage orders had been executed.

Then, after having offered up a prayer of thanksgiving to Jupiter and the other gods for his success, he commanded the victims, which were always white, to be sacrificed; and deposited his golden crown in the lap of the statue of Jupiter, to whom also he dedicated part of the spoils. After this he gave a magnificent entertainment, in the capitol, to his friends and the chief men of the city. After supper he was conducted home by the people with music and a great number of torches. The triumphal procession sometimes took up more than one day; that of Paulus Æmilius, three.

When the victory had been gained at sea, it was called a *naval* triumph, (*triumphus navalis.*)

When a victory had been gained without much difficulty, an inferior kind of triumph, called *ovatio,* was granted, in which the general entered the city on foot or on horseback, crowned with myrtle instead of laurel, and instead of bullocks, sacrificed a sheep.

After the time of Augustus the honor of a triumph was almost entirely confined to the emperors themselves, while the generals only received triumphal ornaments.

The military punishments were of various kinds. The lighter punishments, or such as were attended with inconvenience, loss, or disgrace, were deprivation of pay, forfeiture of their spears, removal from their tent, prohibition from reclining or sitting at meals with the rest, standing before the *prætorium* in a loose jacket, digging in that dress, an allowance of barley instead of wheat, degradation of rank, and dismissal from the camp.   A singular punishment is mentioned by Gellius, namely, that of letting blood.

The more severe punishments were, to be beaten with rods ; to be scourged, and sold as a slave ; to be beaten to death with sticks, which was the usual punishment for theft, desertion, and perjury ; to be stoned ; to be beheaded, sometimes crucified and left unburied ; to be stabbed with the swords of the soldiers ; and, under the emperors, to be exposed to wild beasts or burned alive.

When a number had been guilty of the same crime, as in the case of mutiny, every tenth man was selected for punishment by lot, which was called *decimatio;* or else the ringleaders only were punished.

The Roman soldiers at first received no pay (*stipendium*) from the public, but every one served at his own expense.   Pay was first granted to the soldiers, A. U. 347.   It was, however, very inconsiderable ; two *oboli*, or three *asses* (about 4½ cents) a day to a foot

soldier ; double, to a centurion ; and triple, to
an *eques*. Julius Cæsar doubled the pay. It
was afterwards increased still more.

Besides his pay, each soldier was furnished
with clothes, and received a certain allowance
(*dimensium*) of corn, commonly four bushels a
month ; the centurions, double ; and the *equites*,
triple. But for these things a part of their
pay was deducted. The allies were clothed
and paid by their own states, but received
their allowance of corn from the republic.
The soldiers usually dressed their own victuals,
and took food twice a day, at dinner and
supper.

· When the soldiers had served out their time,
the foot twenty years, and the horse ten, they
were called *emeriti*, and obtained their discharge, (*missia*.)

SECTION VI.

Different kinds of Ships, with their Parts, Ornaments, &c.

It was long before the Romans paid any at-
ention to naval affairs. They at first had
nothing but boats made of thick planks. They
are said to have taken the model of their first
ship of war from a Carthaginian vessel which
happened to be stranded on their coast. But

it is more probable that their first ships of war were built from the model of those of Antium, which, after the reduction of that city, were brought to Rome, A. U. 417.   It was not, however, till the first Punic war, A. U. 497, that they distinguished themselves at sea.

Ships of war were called *naves longæ*, because they were of a longer shape than ships of burden, (*naves onerariæ*,) which were more deep and round.   The ships of war were propelled chiefly by oars, the ships of burden by sails.

The ships of war were variously named from the rows or banks of oars (*ordines remorum*) which they contained.   Those which had two rows were called *biremes;* three, *triremes;* four, *quadremes;* and five, *quinqueremes.*   There were seldom any ships of more than five banks of oars, yet they were sometimes constructed with more than that number, and we read of one which contained sixteen banks.

The rowers were placed one above another in different stages or benches on one side of the ship, not immediately over one another, but in the form of a *quincunx*, thus, :·:·:·:·.   The oars of the lowest bench were short, and those of the other benches increased in length in proportion to their height above the water.

There were three classes of rowers; the first sat in the highest part of the ship, next to the stern; the second, in the middle; the third, in the lowest part of the ship, next to the prow.

Ships contrived for lightness and expedition (*naves actuariæ*) had but one rank of oars on each side, or, at most, two. But the most remarkable of these were the *naves Liburnæ*, a kind of light galleys used by the Liburnians, a people of Dalmatia addicted to piracy. To ships of this kind Augustus was in a great measure indebted for his victory over Antony at Actium. Hence, after that time, the name of *naves Liburnæ* was given to all swiftly-sailing vessels, and most of the ships were built of that construction.

Each ship had a name peculiar to itself, painted on its prow, (called *parasemon*, its sign, or *insigne*,) and as its tutelary god was on its stern, that part of the ship was called *tutela*, and held sacred by the mariners. There supplications and treaties were made.

Ships of burden had a basket suspended to the top of their mast as their sign. There was an ornament in the stern, and sometimes on the prow, made of wood, like the tail of a fish called *aplustre*, from which was erected a staff or pole with a riband or streamer on the top.

The ship of the commander of a fleet was distinguished by a red flag, and by three lights, at night.

The chief parts of a ship and its appendages were *carina*, the heel or bottom; *statu-*

mina, the ribs or pieces of timber which strengthened the sides; *prora,* the prow or fore-part; *puppis,* the stern or hind part; *alveus,* the hold or hollow part; *sentina,* the pump, or rather the bilge or bottom of the hold, where the water which leaked into the ship remained till it was pumped out. In order to keep out the water, ships were covered with wax and pitch, (*ceratæ.*) On the sides (*latera*) were holes (*foramina*) for the oars, (*remi,*) and seats (*sedilia* or *transtra*) for the rowers, (*remiges.*) Each oar was tied to a piece of wood, called *scalmus,* by thongs or strings. The place where the oars were put when the rowers were done working was called *casteria.*

On the stern was the rudder (*gubernaculum*) and the pilot (*gubernator*) who directed it. Some ships had two rudders, one on each end, and two prows, so that they could be propelled either way without turning them.

On the middle of the ship was erected the mast, (*malus,*) which was raised when the ship left the harbor, and taken down when it approached land. On the mast were the sail-yards, (*antennæ,*) and the sails (*vela*) fastened by ropes, (*funes* or *rudentes.*) The sails were usually white, as being thought more lucky, but sometimes colored.

The rigging and tackling of a ship, its sails, oars, ropes, &c., were called *armamenta.*

Ships of war had their prows armed with a

sharp beak (*rostrum*) which usually had three teeth or points.

Ships when about to engage had towers erected on them, whence stones and missive weapons were discharged from engines, called *propugnacula*.

The anchor (*anchora*) was at first of stone, or wood filled with lead, but afterwards of iron. The plummet for sounding depths was called *bolis*. The ropes by which a ship was tied to land were called *retinacula*.

The ballast (*saburra*) was of sand and other heavy substances.

Ships were built of fir, alder, cedar, pine, cypress, and sometimes even of green wood; so that, on one occasion, a number of ships were put on the stocks, completely equipped, and launched, in forty-five days after the timber was cut down in the forest.

There was a place at Rome beyond the Tiber where ships lay and were built, called *navalia*, a dock.

There was great labor in launching the ships, for as the ancients seldom sailed in winter, their ships during that time were drawn up on land. They were drawn to sea by ropes and levers, with rollers placed below.

Section VII.

Mariners, Naval Officers, and Naval Engagements.

As the Romans quickly built fleets, they as speedily manned them. Freedmen and slaves were employed as mariners or rowers, who were called *socii navales*. The citizens and allies were obliged to furnish a certain number of these, according to their fortune.

The legionary soldiers, at first, used to fight at sea as well as on land. But when the Romans came to have regular and constant fleets, there was a separate kind of soldiers raised for the marine service, called *classiarii*, but this service was esteemed less honorable than that of the legionary soldiers. The rowers were occasionally armed.

The admiral of the whole fleet was called *dux classis* or *præfectus classis*, and his ship *navis prætoria*. At first the consuls and prætors commanded the fleets.

The commanders of each ship were called *navarchii;* the master of a trading vessel, *nauclerus*. The person who steered the ship was called *gubernator*, the pilot; sometimes, also, *magister*. He sat at the helm, on the top of the stern, dressed in a particular manner, and gave directions about the management and course of the ship. It was his duty to

know the signs of the weather, to be acquainted with ports and places, and particularly to
observe the winds and stars; for as the ancients knew not the use of the compass, they
were directed in their voyages in the night time
by the stars, and in the day by the coasts and
islands which they knew, so that they did not
dare to venture far from land.

The *hortator* or *pausarius* had command over
the rowers. The *helciarii* were those who
hauled or pulled the ropes. These animated
one another with a loud cry, (*nauticus clamor*.)

Before a fleet (*classis*) set out to sea, it was
solemnly reviewed like an army, prayers were
made, and victims sacrificed, auspices consulted; and if any unlucky omen happened, as a
person sneezing on the left, or swallows alight-
ing on the ships, the voyage was suspended.

The mariners when they set sail or reached
the harbor, decked their stern with garlands.

The signal for embarking was given with
the trumpet. They embarked in a certain order, the mariners first, and then the soldiers.
They also sailed in a certain order, the light
vessels foremost, then the fleet or ships of war,
and after them the ships of burden. They
consulted the omens as they approached the
place of their destination, in the same manner
as at their departure. When they reached
the shore, and landed the troops, prayers and
sacrifices were again made.

Harbors (*portus*) were strongly fortified, especially at the entrance. There was usually a watch-tower (*pharos*) with lights to direct the course of ships in the night time.

Fleets about to engage in battle, were arranged in a manner similar to armies on land. Certain ships were placed in the centre, others in the right wing, and others in the left, and some as a reserve. They were generally disposed in the form of a semicircle.

Before the engagement, sacrifices and prayers were offered, and the admiral sailed round the fleet in a light galley, and exhorted the men. The soldiers and sailors made ready for action, by furling the sails and adjusting the rigging, for they never chose to fight but in calm weather. A red flag was displayed from the ship of the admiral as a signal to engage. The trumpets in all the ships were sounded, and a shout raised by all the crews.

The combatants endeavored to sink or disable the ships of the enemy by sweeping off the oars, or by striking them with their beaks. They grappled with them by means of certain machines called crows, (*corvi*,) iron hooks, (*ferreæ manus*,) grappling irons, (*harpagones ;*) and fought as on land. They sometimes employed fire-ships or threw firebrands and pots filled with sulphur, coals, and other combustibles.

In sieges they joined vessels together, and erected on them various engines; or sunk vessels to block up their harbors.

The ships of the victorious fleet when they returned home had their prows decked with laurel and resounded with triumphant music.

The prizes distributed after a victory at sea were much the same as on land ; also naval punishments, provisions, &c.

The trading vessels of the ancients were in general much inferior in size to those of the moderns. A number are mentioned which were considered large, and which were of about fifty-six tons burden. There were, however, some ships of enormous bulk.

CHAPTER IV.

RELIGION OF THE ROMANS.

SECTION I.

Roman Deities, and Sacred Places.

THE religion of the Romans was idolatry in its grossest and most extensive acceptation. Their gods were very numerous, and divided into the great celestial deities (*Dii Majorum gentium*) and the inferior deities, (*Dii Minorum gentium.*) The great celestial deities were twelve in number, Jupiter, Neptune, Mars, Apollo, Vulcan, Mercury, who were masculine deities; and Juno, Minerva, or Pallas, Venus, Ceres, Diana, and Vesta, who were feminine.

Among the great celestial deities were also included the select deities, (*dii selecti*,) who were eight in number.*

The inferior deities were of various kinds. The *Dii Indigetes* were heroes, ranked among the gods on account of their virtues and merits. The *Semones* were inferior deities, superior to men and inferior to gods, as the word (*semi homines*, half-men) indicates.

The Romans also worshipped the virtues and affections of the mind, as *Piety, Faith, Hope, Concord, Fame, &c.*, even vices and diseases; and under the emperors, foreign deities, as *Isis, Osiris, Anubis*, of the Egyptians; also the winds and tempests.

They worshipped certain gods that they might do them good, and others that they might not harm them.   There was both a good and bad Jupiter; the former was called *Dijovis* or *Diespiter ;* the latter, *Vejovis* or *Vedius.*

The places dedicated to the worship of the gods were called temples, (*templa, fana, delubra, sacraria, œdes sacrœ*,) and consecrated by the Augurs.   A temple built by Augustus, and dedicated to all the gods, was called *Pantheon*.

---

* For a description of these and other deities of the Greeks and Romans, see the mythology at the end of this work.

A small temple or chapel was called *sacel lum* or *ædicula*. A wood or thicket of trees consecrated to religious worship was called *lucus*, a grove. The gods were supposed to frequent woods and fountains.

The walls of cities were considered sacred, but not the gates. The gates, however, were esteemed inviolable, (*sancta.*)

A place was held sacred where a dead body was buried, but not where it was burned.

Altars and temples afforded an asylum or place of refuge among the Romans, as well as most other ancient nations; chiefly to slaves from the cruelty of their masters, and to insolvent debtors and criminals, when it was considered impious to touch them; but sometimes they put fire and combustible materials around the place, that the person might appear to be forced away, not by men, but by a god, or shut up the temple and unroofed it, that he might perish in the open air.

Section II.

Ministers of Religion.

The ministers of religion (*ministri sacrorum*) among the Romans did not form a distinct order from the other citizens. They were usually chosen from the most honorable men in the state. Some of them were common to all the gods ; others the priests of a particular deity.

The *pontifices* judged in all cases relating to sacred things ; and in cases where there was no written law, they prescribed what regulations they thought proper. Their authority was very great. It particularly belonged to them to see that the inferior priests did their duty. The whole number of *pontifices* was called *collegium.* This number, at first, consisted of four, but afterwards increased to fifteen.

The chief of the *pontifices* was called *Pontifex Maximus,* high priest. He was created by the people, while the other pontifices were chosen by the college. The *pontifex maximus* was an office of great dignity and power. He was supreme judge and arbiter in all religious matters. All the other priests were subject to him. He could hinder any of them from leaving the city.

The presence of the *pontifex maximus* was requisite in public and solemn religious acts, as when magistrates vowed games, &c. He attended at the *comitia ;* especially when priests were created, that he might inaugurate them.

The *pontifex maximus* and his college judged concerning marriages, and had the care of regulating the year and the public calendar.

For a long time the *pontifex maximus* drew

up a short account of the public transactions of every year, in a book, and exposed this register in an open place in his house, where the people might come and read it. These records were called *annales*, or *commentarii*.

The *pontifices* wore a robe bordered with purple, a woollen cap in the form of a cone, with a small rod wrapped round with wool, and a tuft or tassel on the top of it, called *apex*.

In ancient times the *pontifex maximus* was not permitted to leave Italy. This office was for life.

The *Augures*, augurs or soothsayers, were at first three in number, but were afterwards increased to fifteen. Their office was to explain all omens, foretell future events from the flight, chirping, or feeding of birds, and other appearances. They were a college of priests of the greatest authority at Rome, because nothing of importance was done respecting the public, either at home or abroad, in peace or in war, without consulting them. The chief of the augurs was called *magister collegii*.

The augurs enjoyed this singular privilege, that of whatever crime they were guilty, they could not be deprived of their offices, because they were intrusted with the secrets of the empire.

The badges of the augurs were, a kind of robe, (*trabea*,) striped with purple, a cap of conical shape, like that of the pontifices, and a crooked staff, which they carried in their right hand to mark out the quarters of the heavens.

An augur made his observations on the heavens usually in the dead of night, or else about twilight.

The *Haruspices* examined the victims and their entrails, after they were sacrificed, and thus derived omens of futurity, as well as from the smoke, flame, and other circumstances attending the sacrifice ; as if the victim came to the altar without resistance, stood there quietly, fell by one stroke, bled freely, &c. These were favorable signs. They also explained prodigies. Their office resembled that of the augurs, but they were not esteemed so honorable. Of what number the college of *haruspices* consisted is uncertain. Their chief was called *summus haruspex.*

Quindecemviri were, as their name imports, *fifteen* in number. They had charge of the Sibylline books, inspected them by the appointment of the senate in dangerous conjunctures ; and performed the sacrifices which they enjoined. It belonged to them in particular to celebrate the secular games, and those of Apollo. They are said to have been instituted on the following occasion.

A certain woman, named Amalthæa, from a foreign country, is said to have come to Tarquin the Proud, wishing to sell nine books of Sibylline, or prophetic oracles. But upon Tarquin's refusal to give her the price which

K

she asked, she went away and burned three of them. Returning soon after, she demanded the same price for the remaining six. Whereupon being ridiculed by the king, as a senseless old woman, she went and burned three more; and coming back still demanded the same price for the three which remained. Tarquin, surprised at the strange conduct of the woman, consulted the augurs what to do. They, regretting the loss of the books which had been destroyed, advised the king to give the price required. The woman, therefore, having delivered the books, and having desired that they should be carefully kept, disappeared and was never afterwards seen. Tarquin committed the care of these Sibylline books (*libri sibyllini*) to two men appointed for this purpose, and these were subsequently increased to fifteen.

The chief of the *quindecemviri* was called *magister collegii.*

These sibylline books were supposed to contain the fate of the Roman empire, and therefore in public danger or calamity, the keepers of them were frequently ordered by the senate to inspect them. They were kept in a stone chest below ground in the temple of Jupiter in the Capitol. But the Capitol being burned in the Marsic war, A. U. 670, these books were destroyed with it; whereupon ambassadors were sent everywhere to collect the oracles of the Sibyls. From the various Sibylline verses thus collected the *quindecemviri* made out new books.

The *quindecemviri* were exempted from the obligation of serving in the army, and from other offices in the city. Their priesthood was for life.

The *Septemviri* prepared the sacred feasts at games, processions, and on other solemn occasions.

The *Pontifices, Augures, Septemviri,* and *Quindecemviri* were called " the four colleges of priests."

The other fraternities of priests were less considerable, although composed of persons of distinguished rank.

The *Fratres Ambavales,* twelve in number, offered up sacrifices for the fertility of the ground. Their office was for life, and continued even in captivity and exile. They wore a crown made of the ears of corn, and a white woollen wreath around their temples.

The *Curiones* were priests who performed the public sacred rites, in each *curia,* thirty in number.

The *Feciales** were priests employed in declaring war and concluding peace. The *Fecialis,* who took the oath in the name of the Roman people in concluding a treaty of peace, was called *Pater Patratus.* The number of the *Feciales* is supposed to have been twenty. They judged concerning every thing which

* See Chap. III. Sec. I.

related to the proclaiming of war and the making of treaties. They were sent to the enemy to demand redress of injuries. They always carried in their hands, or wreathed round their temples, vervain, a kind of sacred grass, plucked from a particular place in the Capitol, in which it grew.

The *Sodales* were priests appointed to preserve the sacred rites of the Sabines.

The *Rex Sacrorum* was a priest appointed after the expulsion of Tarquin to perform those sacred rites which the kings themselves had before performed,—an office of small importance, and subject to the *pontifex maximus*, as all the other priesthoods were. Before a person was admitted to this priesthood he was obliged to resign any other office he bore. His wife was called *Regina*, or queen.

The priests of particular gods were called *Flamines.* The chief of these were, the *Flamen Dialis*, the priest of Jupiter, who was distinguished by a lictor, and had a right from his office of coming into the senate; the *Flamen Martialis*, the priest of wars; and *Flamen Quirinalis*, the priest of Romulus. The *Flamines* wore a purple robe called *læna*, and a conical cap.

The Flamen of Jupiter was an office of great dignity, but subjected to many restrictions, as that he should not ride on horseback, nor stay one night without the city, nor take an oath. His wife (*flaminica*) was also under particular restrictions, and could not be divorced; and when she died, the *flamen* resigned his office, because he could not perform certain rites without her assistance.

The *Salii* were the priests of Mars, twelve in number, so called because on solemn occasions they went through the city *dancing*, dressed in an embroidered tunic, bound with a brazen belt and a *toga prætexta*, having on their head a high conical cap, with a sword by their side, a spear in their right hand, and one of the *ancilia*, or shields of Mars, in their left. They went through the public parts of the city singing sacred songs.

The *Luperci* were priests of Pan, so called from *lupus*, a wolf, because Pan was the god who was supposed to keep the wolves from the sheep. The place where he was worshipped was called *Lupercal*, and his festival *Lupercalia*, which was celebrated in February, at which time the *Luperci* ran up and down the city nearly naked, having thongs in their hands, with which they struck those whom they met.

The *Potitii* and *Pinarii* were priests of Hercules: the former presided at the sacrifices of Hercules; the latter acted as assistants.

The *Galli* were the priests of *Cybele*, the mother of the gods. They were called also *Curetes*, and *Corybantes*, and their chief, *Archigallus*. They carried round the image of Cybele, with the gestures of mad people, rolling their heads, beating their breasts to the sound of their flute, drums, and cymbals, cutting their arms, and uttering dreadful predictions. They annually went round the villages asking alms, which all other priests were prohibited from doing. The rites of Cybele were disgraced by great indecency of expression.

The *Virgines Vestales*, vestal virgins, were consecrated to the worship of Vesta, at first four in number, afterwards six. They were selected for admission between the ages of six and sixteen years, and were to be free from any bodily defect, and their parents must be alive and free-born citizens. They were bound to their ministry for thirty years. For the first ten they learned the sacred rites; for the next ten they performed them; and for the last ten they taught the younger virgins. After this they might leave the temple and marry, which, however, was seldom done.

The office of the vestal virgins was to keep the sacred fire always burning, watching it in the night-time alternately, and whoever allowed it to go out, was scourged by the *pontifex maximus*, or by his order. This accident was always esteemed unlucky, and expiated by offering extraordinary sacrifices. The fire was rekindled, not from another fire, but from the rays of the sun, in which manner it was renewed every year on the first of March. These vestals also kept the secret pledge of the empire, supposed to have been the *Palla-*

dium, or the *Penates* of the Roman people kept in the innermost recess of the temple, and visible only to the *Vestalis maxima.* The Vestal Virgins wore a long white robe bordered with purple, their head decorated with fillets and ribands. They enjoyed singular honors and privileges. The consuls and prætors, when they met them in the street, lowered their *fasces,* and went out of their way to show them respect. They could free a criminal from punishment if they met him accidentally. Deeds and wills were committed to their care.

If any Vestal violated her vow of chastity, after being tried and sentenced by the *Pontifices* she was buried alive with funeral solemnities, and her paramour scourged to death in the Forum.

The priests who had children, employed them to assist in performing sacred rites; but those who had no children, procured free-born boys and girls to serve them. Those who took care of the temples were called *Æditui;* those who brought the victims to the altar and slew them, *Popæ.*

Section III.

Religious Rites, Prayers, Vows, Sacrifices, Purifications, and Oaths.

The Romans were, as a people, remarkably attached to their religion, and scrupulously attentive to its rites and ceremonies.

The worship (*cultus*) of the gods consisted chiefly in prayers, vows, and sacrifices.

No act of religious worship was performed without prayer, (*oratio, precatio, preces.*) The words were thought of the greatest importance, and varied according to the nature of the sacrifice. In the day-time the gods were supposed to remain in heaven, but to go up and down the earth during the night, to observe the actions of men. The stars were supposed to do the contrary. Those who prayed to the gods, stood usually with their heads covered, looking towards the east ; a priest pronounced the words before them ; they frequently touched the altars or the knees of the images of the gods, turning themselves round in a circle, and also prostrated themselves on the ground.

With the same solemnity they offered up vows, (*vota.*) They vowed temples, games, sacrifices, gifts, a certain part of the plunder of a city, &c., also what was called *ver sacrum*, that is, all the cattle which were produced from the first of March to the end of April. Sometimes they wrote their vows, and sealed them up, and fastened them with wax to the knees of the images of the gods; that place being supposed to be the seat of mercy.

The person who made vows was bound, when he obtained his wish, to make good his vow. Those saved from shipwreck hung up their clothes in the temple of Neptune, with a picture (*tabula votiva*) representing the circumstances of their danger and escape. So soldiers, when discharged, suspended their arms to Mars; gladiators their swords to Hercules; and poets, when they finished a work, the fillets of their hair to Apollo.

Thanksgivings (*gratiarum actiones*) were always made to the gods for benefits received, and upon all fortunate events. When a general had gained a signal victory, a thanksgiving (*supplicatio*) was decreed by the senate to be made in all the temples, and what was called *lectisternium*, when couches were spread for the gods, as if about to feast, and their images taken down from their pedestals, and placed upon these couches around the altars, which were loaded with the richest dishes.

In sacrifices (*sacrificia*) it was necessary that those who offered them should come chaste and pure; that they should bathe themselves, be dressed in white robes, and crowned with the leaves of that tree which was thought most acceptable to the god whom they wor-

L

shipped. Sometimes they came in the garb of suppliants, with dishevelled hair, loose robes, and barefooted. Vows and prayers were always made before the sacrifice.

It was necessary that the animals to be sacrificed (*hostiæ* or *victimæ*) should be without spot and blemish, never yoked for labor, and chosen from a flock or herd approved by the priests, and marked with chalk. They were adorned with fillets, ribands, and crowns, and their horns were gilded.

The victim was led to the altar by the *popæ*, with their clothes tucked up, and naked to the waist. The animal was led by a slack rope, that it might not seem to be brought by force, which was reckoned a bad omen. For the same reason it was allowed to stand loose before the altar, and it was a very bad omen if it fled away. Then after silence was ordered, a salted cake (*mola salta* or *fruges saltæ*) was sprinkled on the head of the beast, and frankincense and wine (*libatio*) poured between its horns, the priest having first tasted the wine himself, and given it to be tasted by those that stood near to him. The priest plucked the highest hairs between the horns, and threw them into the fire. The victim was struck by the *cultrarius*, with an axe or mallet, (*malleus*,) by the order of the priest. Then it was stabbed with knives, and the blood being caught in goblets, was poured on the altar. It was then flayed and dissected. Sometimes it was all burned and called *holocaustum,* but usually only a paﬅ; what remained was divided between the priest and the person who offered the sacrifice.

The *haruspices* inspected the entrails, and if the signs were favorable they were said to have offered up an acceptable sacrifice, or to have pacified the gods ; if not, another victim was offered up, and sometimes several.

The liver was the part chiefly inspected, and supposed to give the most certain presages of futurity. It was divided into two parts, called *pars familiaris* and *pars hostilis.* From the former they conjectured what was to happen to themselves, and from the latter what was to happen to an enemy.

After the *haruspices* had inspected the entrails, the parts which fell to the gods were sprinkled with meal, wine, and frankincense, and burned on the altar ; or when in sacrificing to marine deities, they were thrown into the sea.

When the sacrifice was finished, the priest having washed his hands and uttered certain prayers, again made a libation, and then the people were dismissed in a set form of words. After the sacrifice followed a feast.

The sacrifices offered to the celestial gods differed from those offered to the infernal deities in several particulars. The victims sacrificed to the former were white, their neck was bent upward, the knife was applied from

above, and the blood was sprinkled on the altar
or caught in goblets; the victims offered to the
infernal gods were black, they were killed with
their faces bent downward, (*pronæ*,) the knife
was applied from below, and the blood was
poured into a ditch.   Those who sacrificed
to the celestial gods were clothed in white,
bathed the whole body, made libations by pouring the liquor out of the cup, and prayed with
the palms of their hands raised to heaven;
those who sacrificed to the infernal gods were
clothed in black, only sprinkled their body with
water, made libations by turning the hands,
and threw the cups into the fire, and prayed
with their palms turned downward, and striking the ground with their feet.

Human sacrifices were sometimes offered
among the Romans.   By an ancient law, persons guilty of certain crimes, treachery or sedition, were devoted to Pluto and the infernal
gods; and therefore any one might slay them
with impunity.   Men were sometimes thrown
into the sea, as victims to Neptune.

A place reared for offering sacrifices was
called *ara* or *altare*, an altar.   A secret place
in the temple, where none but the priests entered, was called *adytum*.

At the time when the censors had finished
the census, an expiatory or purifying sacrifice
was made of a sow, a sheep, and a bull, which
were carried round the whole assembly, and
then slain; thus the people were said to be

purified. This sacrifice was called *suovetau-rilia.*

At funerals, also, when the remains of the deceased were laid in the tomb, those present were three times sprinkled by a priest with pure water, from a branch of olive or laurel, to purify them. There were many other purifications among the Romans.

The Romans in solemn oaths (*jurajuranda*) held a flint-stone in their right hand, and invited awful imprecations upon themselves if they perjured themselves. The most solemn oath of the Romans was by their faith or honor.

The *sacramentum* was the solemn military oath.

Section IV.

Divination and Augury.

The difference between the terms divination (*divinatio*) and augury (*augurium*) is, that the former is general and indefinite, while the latter is specific and has its fixed reasons. But this distinction is not always clearly made by the ancient authors.

The tokens (*signæ*) of futurity were chiefly derived from five sources—1. From appearances in the heavens, as thunder, lightning, meteors, as for instance whether the thunder came from the right or left ;—2. From the singing or chattering of birds, as the raven, the crow, owl, cock ; and the flying of others, as the eagle, vulture, &c. ;—3. From the manner in which chickens fed, as, if they did not eat voraciously, it was esteemed an unfortunate omen ;— 4. From beasts crossing the way, or appearing in a strange place ;—5. From unusual accidents, such as sneezing, stumbling, spilling salt upon the table, &c.

To take the auguries from appearances in the heavens, or from birds, the augur took his station on an elevated place, (*arx*,) offered up sacrifices, uttered a solemn prayer, with his head covered, and his face turned to the east, and with his rod (*lituus*) determined the regions of the heavens from east to west, and then awaited the omen.

Among the Romans, omens on the left were generally esteemed lucky, but not always ; while the Greeks considered the right as the propitious quarter.

Future events were also prognosticated by drawing lots, (*sortes ;*) by observing the stars, (*astrologia* or *Babylonica doctrina ;*) by interpreting dreams, (*conjectura somniorum,*) &c. Persons disordered in their mind were supposed to possess the faculty of presaging future events.

The auspices either of appearances in the heavens, or inspection of birds, were always taken at the time of the *comitia ;* as also sometimes that of feeding chickens. And so scrupulous were the ancient Romans about this matter, that if the augurs, at any time afterwards, upon recollection, declared that there had been any informality in taking the auspices, the magistrates who had been at that time elected, were obliged to resign their office, even several months after they had entered upon it.

———

Section V.

Festivals of the Romans.

Days among the Romans were either dedicated to religious purposes, (*dies festi,*) or assigned to ordinary business, (*dies profesti.*) There were some days in which a part was devoted to one and a part to the other, called *dies intersici,* 'half holidays.' On the *dies festi,* sacrifices were performed, feasts and games were celebrated, or at least there was a cessation from business.

Public *Feriæ,* or festivals, were either stated (*statæ*) or annually fixed on a certain day, by the magistrates or priests, (*conceptivæ,*) or occasionally appointed by the consul, prætor, or *pontifex maximus,* (*imperativæ.*)

The stated festivals were chiefly the following :—

1. In January, *Agonalia*, in honor of Janus, on the 9th, and also on the 20th of May; *Carmentalia*, on the 11th. This was a half holiday.

2. In February, *Faunalia*, to the god Faunus, on the 13th; *Lupercalia*, to Pan, on the 15th; *Quirinalia*, to Romulus, on the 17th; *Feralia*, on the 21st; *Regifugium*, in commemoration of the flight of king Tarquin, on the 24th; *Equiria*, horse-races, in the Campus Martius, in honor of Mars, on the 27th.

3. In March, *Matronalia*, celebrated by the matrons on the first day, when presents were given by husbands to their wives; *Testum Anciliorum*, on the same day and three following, when the shields of Mars were carried through the city by the *Salii; Liberalia*, to Bacchus, on the 18th, when young men first assumed the *toga virilis*, or manly gown; *Quinquetrus*, in honor of Minerva, on the 19th, continuing for five days; *Hilaria*, in honor of the mother of the gods, on the 25th.

4. In April, *Megalesia*, to the great mother of the gods, on the 4th or 5th; *Cerealia*, to Ceres, on the 9th; *Fordicidia*, on the 15th, when pregnant cows were sacrificed; *Palilia*, to Pales, on the 21st, on which day the city of Rome was founded; *Robigalia*, to Robigus, that he would preserve the corn from mildew on the 25th; *Floralia*, to Flora, begun on the 28th, and continued to the end of the month, attended with great indecency.

5. In May, on the Kalends (or first day) were performed the sacred rites of the *Bona Dea*, by the Vestal Virgins and women only, in the house of the consul and prætors, for the safety of the people ; *Compitalia*, to the Lares in the public ways, in which boys were anciently sacrificed to Mania, the mother of the Lares, on the 2d ; *Lemuria*, on the 9th, to the *Lemures*, ghosts or spectres in the dark, which were believed to be the souls of their deceased friends ; *Festum mercatorum*, the festival of the merchants, when they offered sacred rites to Mercury, on the 13th ; *Vulcanalia*, in honor of Vulcan, on the 22d..

6. In June, on the Kalends, were the festivals of the goddess Carna ; of Mars *Extramuraneus*, whose temple was without the walls ; and of Juno *Moneta ;* on the 4th, of Bellona ; on the 7th, *Ludi Piscatorii ;* on the 9th, *Vestalia*, to Vesta ; on the 10th, *Matralia*.

7. In July, on the Kalends, people removed from hired lodgings ; on the 4th was the festival of *Female Fortune*, in memory of Coriolanus withdrawing his army from the city ; on the 5th, *Ludi Appollinares ;* on the 12th, the birth-day of Julius Cæsar ; on the 15th, the grand procession of the *Equites ;* on the 16th, *Dies allieais*, on which the Romans were defeated by the Gauls ; on the 23d, *Neptunalia*, to Neptune.

8. In August, on the 13th, the festival of Diana ; on the 19th, *Vinalia*, when a libation of

new wine was made to Jupiter and Venus;
on the 18th, *Consualia*, games in honor of Con-
sus, the god of council, or of *Equestrian* Neptune, at which the Sabine women were carried off by the Romans ; on the 23d, *Vulcanalia*, to Vulcan.

9. In September, on the 4th, *Ludi magni* or
Romani, in honor of the *great* gods, Jupiter,
Juno, and Minerva, for the safety of the city ;
on the 13th, the consul or dictator used anciently to fix a nail in the temple of Jupiter,
which is supposed to have been done to mark
the number of years ; on the 30th, *Meditrina-
lia*, to Meditrina, the goddess of curing or heal-
ing, at which time new wine was first drunk.

10. In October, on the 12th, *Augustalia*, or
Ludi Augustales; on the 13th, *Faunalia;* on
the 15th, a horse was sacrificed, called *Equus
Octobris*, because Troy was supposed to have
been taken in this month by means of a horse.
The tail was brought with great speed to the
Regia or house of the *pontifex maximus*, that
its blood might drop on the hearth.

11. In November, on the 13th, there was a
sacred feast, called *Epulum Jovis ;* on the 27th,
sacred rites were performed on account of two
Greeks and two Gauls, a man and a woman
of each, who were buried alive in the ox-mar-
ket, in compliance with the oracles found in
the books of the Sibyls, at the beginning of the
Gallic war, and also at the beginning of the
second Punic war.

12. In December, on the 5th, *Faunalia ;* on the 17th, *Saturnalia*, the feasts of Saturn, the most celebrated of the whole year, when all ranks were devoted to mirth and feasting, friends sent presents to one another, and masters treated their slaves as their equals, and even served them at table. This feast continued at first for one day, afterwards for three, and then for five ; on the 23d, *Laurentinalia*, in honor of *Laurentia Acca*, the wife of the shepherd Faustulus, and nurse of Romulus.

The *Feriæ Conceptivæ*, which were annually appointed by the magistrates, were—

1. *Feriæ Latinæ*, the Latin holidays, which were solemnized by the Latins in common with the Romans, on the Alban mountain, at first for one day, afterwards for four days.

2. *Paganalia*, celebrated in the villages to the tutelary gods of the rustic tribes, at which time every peasant should pay into the hands of the censor a piece of money, the men a piece of one kind, the women of another, and the children of a third kind ; and in this way the number of inhabitants was taken.

3. *Sementivæ*, in seed-time, for a good crop.

4. *Compitalia*, to the *Lares*, in places where several ways met.

Feriæ Imperativæ were holidays appointed occasionally, as when it was said to have rained stones, for expiating other prodigies, on account of some public calamity, or of some victory.

Feriæ were sometimes private, and celebra
ted only in families, on the birth-day of some
member or ancestor, &c.

As most of the year was taken up in holidays and sacrifices, to the great loss of the
public, the emperor Claudius abridged their
number.

CHAPTER V.

PUBLIC GAMES, AND AMUSEMENTS OF THE ROMANS.

Section I.

The Games and Shows of the Circus ; Athletic Exercises, &c.

Games among the Romans constituted a part
of religious worship. At first, they were always consecrated to some god. The most famous games were those celebrated in the
Circus Maximus. This *circus* was built by Tarquinius Priscus, and afterwards at different
times magnificently adorned. It was situated
between the Palatine and Aventine hills, and
was of an oblong circular form ; its length was

730 yards, or about three sevenths of a mile;
the breadth about one third of the length, with
seats all around rising one above another. It
is said to have contained 150,000 persons, or
according to others, double that number. Its
circumference was a mile. On one end there
were several openings, from which the horses
and chariots started, called *carceres*.

The shows (*spectacula*) exhibited in the *Circus Maximus*, were chiefly the following:

1. Chariot and horse-races, of which the
Romans were extravagantly fond. The charioteers (*agitatores* or *aurigæ*) were distributed
into four parties, distinguished by their different dress or livery,—the white, (*albata;*) the red,
(*russata;*) the blue or sea-colored, (*veneta;*)
and the green, (*prasina;*) to which Domitian
added two, the golden, (*aurata,*) and the purple,
(*purpurea.*) The spectators favored one or the
other color, as humor or caprice inclined them.

The order in which the chariots stood was
determined by lot; and the person who presided at the games gave the signal for starting
by dropping a napkin or cloth. A trumpet
also sounded. Then they sprang forward, and
whoever first ran seven times round the course
was victorious. The victor being proclaimed
by the voice of a herald, was crowned, and
received a prize in money of considerable value. Palms were also given to the victors.

2. Contests of agility and strength, of which
there were five kinds; running, (*cursus;*) leap-

ing, (*saltus ;*) boxing, (*pugilatus ;*) wrestling, (*lucta ;*) and throwing the *discus* or quoit, (*disci jactus.*)　In these exercises the combatants (*athletæ*) contended nearly naked, with no clothing but drawers.　This covering, which went from the waist downward, and supplied the place of a tunic, was called *campestre*, and the place for exercises, *gymnasium.*

The *Athletæ* were anointed with a glutinous ointment, (*ceroma.*) Boxers covered their hands with a kind of gloves, (*chirothecæ,*) which had lead or iron sewed in them, to make the strokes fall with greater weight.

The *athletæ* were previously trained in a place of exercise, and restricted to a particular diet.

3. *Ludus Trojæ,* a mock-fight performed by young noblemen on horseback.

4. *Venatio,* or the fighting of wild beasts with one another, or with men called *bestiarii,* who were either forced to this by way of punishment, as the primitive Christians often were, or fought voluntarily, either from a natural ferocity of disposition, or induced by hire.　An incredible number of wild animals of various kinds were brought from all quarters for the entertainment of the people, and at an immense expense.　They were kept in enclosures (*vivaria*) till the day of exhibition.　Pompey exhibited at one time five hundred lions; at another time one hundred and forty-two elephants were procured ; and besides lions, ele-

phants, bears, &c., one hundred and fifty pan-
thers were shown at one time.

5. The representation of a horse and foot
battle, and also of an encampment, or a siege.

6. The representation of a sea-fight, (*nau-
machia*,) which was at first made in the *Circus
Maximus*, but more frequently elsewhere.
Augustus dug a lake near the Tiber for that
purpose ; and Domitian built a naval Theatre.
Those who fought were called *naumachiarii*.
They were usually composed of captives, or
condemned malefactors, who fought to death
unless saved by the clemency of the emperor.

If any thing unlucky happened at the
games, they were renewed, and often more
than once.

Section II.

Gladiatorial Shows.

The shows of gladiators were properly
called *Munera*, and the person who exhibited
them *Munerarius ;* who, although in a private
station, enjoyed, during the days of the exhibition, the ensigns of magistracy.

Gladiators were first publicly exhibited at
Rome by two brothers, named *Bruti*, at the
funeral of their father ; and for some time
they were exhibited only on such occasions

but afterwards also by the magistrates, to entertain the people, chiefly at the *Saturnalia,* and feasts of Minerva. Incredible numbers of men were destroyed in this manner. After the triumph of Trajan over the Dacians, spectacles were exhibited for one hundred and twenty-three days, in which eleven thousand animals of different kinds were killed, and ten thousand gladiators fought.

Gladiators were kept and maintained in schools by persons called *Lanistæ,* who purchased and trained them. When they exercised, they fenced with wooden swords. They were at first composed of captives and slaves, or condemned malefactors. But afterwards also free-born citizens, induced by hire or inclination, fought on the *arena ;* some even of noble birth ; and, what is still more wonderful, women of rank.

Gladiators were distinguished by their armor and manner of fighting. The *secutores* had for their arms, a helmet, a shield, and a sword, or leaden bullet. The *Retiarii* were usually matched with them. These were dressed in a short tunic, with the head bare, bearing in their left hand a three-pointed lance, and in their right a net, (*retis,*) with which they attempted to entangle their adversary, by casting it over his head and suddenly drawing it together, and then slaying him with their trident. But if the *retiarius* missed his aim, either by throwing his net too short or too far, he instantly betook himself to flight, and endeavored to prepare his net for a second cast; while his antagonist as quickly pursued (whence the name, *secutor*) to prevent his design by dispatching him.

The gladiators sometimes fought in numbers and sometimes in pairs. They were generally exhibited in an amphitheatre.

The largest amphitheatre was begun by Vespasian and completed by Titus, now called *Colisæum*. It was of an oval form, and could contain 87,000 spectators. Its ruins still remain. The place where the gladiators fought was called *arena*, because it was covered with *sand*, or saw-dust, to prevent the gladiators from sliding, and to absorb the blood. The *podium* was next the *arena*, where the senators and ambassadors of foreign nations sat. The *podium* projected over the wall which surrounded the *arena*, and was raised between twelve and fifteen feet above it, secured with a breast-work against the irruption of wild beasts. As a further defence, the *arena* was surrounded with an iron railing and a canal. The *Equites* sat behind the senators, and the rest of the people behind the *Equites*.

Anciently women were not permitted to see the gladiators, but afterwards this restriction was removed.

Nigh to the amphitheatre was a place called *spoliarium*, to which those who were killed, or mortally wounded, were dragged by a hook.

M

On the day of the exhibition the gladiators were led along the *arena* in procession. Then they were matched by pairs, and their swords were examined by the exhibitor of the games. As a prelude to battles, they first fought with wooden swords, flourishing their arms with great dexterity. Then, upon a signal given, with a trumpet, they laid aside these, and assumed their proper arms. They adjusted themselves with great care, and stood in a particular posture. They then pushed at one another, and repeated the thrust. As it was more easy to parry or avoid direct thrusts than back or side strokes, they took particular care to defend their side.

When any gladiator was wounded, the spectators exclaimed ' *habet*,' (he has got it.) The gladiator lowered his arms, as a sign of his being vanquished; but his fate depended on the pleasure of the people, who, if they wished him to be saved, pressed down their thumbs; if to be slain, they turned up their thumbs, and ordered him to receive the sword, which gladiators usually submitted to with amazing fortitude.

. The rewards given to the victors were a palm, money, and a reed or wooden sword, as a sign of their being discharged from fighting.

The spectators expressed the same eagerness by wagers (*sponsiones*) on the different gladiators as in the *Circus*.

SECTION III.

The Theatre and Drama.

Dramatic entertainments were first introduced at Rome on account of a pestilence, A. U. 391, to appease the divine wrath. Before that time there had been only the games of the *circus*. They were called *ludi scenici*, because they were first acted in a shade, formed by branches and leaves of trees; hence afterwards the front of the theatre, where the actors stood, was called *scena*, and the actors *scenici*.

Rude plays, made up with music, dancing, and buffoonery, were in use in the earlier periods of the republic; but afterwards the entertainment was improved, and a new kind of dramatic composition was contrived, called *satyræ* or *saturæ*, 'satires.' These satires were set to music, and repeated with suitable gestures, accompanied with the flute and dancing. They contained much ridicule and smart rapartee.

It was Livius Andronicus, the freedman of M. Livius Salinator, and the preceptor of his sons, who, giving up satires, first ventured to write a regular play about A. U. 512. He was the actor of his own compositions, as all then were. Being obliged by the audience frequently to repeat the same part, and thus becoming hoarse, he obtained permission to employ a boy to sing to the flute, while he acted what was sung.

Plays were afterwards greatly improved at Rome from the model of the Greeks.

Dramatic entertainments, in their improved state, were chiefly of three kinds, *Comedy*, *Tragedy*, and *Pantomimes*.

1. Comedy (*Comœdia*) was a representation of common life, written in a familiar style, and usually with a happy issue. The design of it was to expose vice and folly to ridicule.

Comedy among the Greeks was divided into old, middle, and new. In the first, real characters and names were represented ; in the second, real characters, but fictitious names; in the third, both fictitious characters and names. Nothing was ever known at Rome but the new comedy.

Comedies among the Romans were distinguished by the character and dress of the persons introduced on the stage. The actors of comedy wore a low-heeled shoe, called *soccus*.

2. Tragedy (*tragœdia*) is said to have been invented by Thespis, a native of Attica, about 536 years before Christ. He went about in Greece, with his actors, from village to village, in a cart, on which a temporary stage was erected, where they played and sang, having their faces smeared with the lees of wine. Thespis was succeeded by Æschylus, who erected a permanent stage, and was the in-

ventor of the mask, of the long-flowing robe, and of the high-heeled shoe or buskin (*cothurnus*) which tragedians wore. After Æschylus followed Sophocles and Euripides, who brought tragedy to the highest perfection. In their time, comedy began first to be considered as a distinct composition from tragedy: but at Rome comedy was long cultivated before any attempt was made to compose tragedies. The tragedy represented some signal action, performed by illustrious persons, and generally having a fatal issue.

Every regular play among the Romans was divided into five acts : the subdivision into scenes is thought to be a modern invention.

Between the acts of a tragedy were introduced a number of singers, (*chorus.*) The music chiefly used was that of the flute, of which instrument there were various forms.

3. Pantomimes (*pantomimi*) were representations by dumb show, in which the actors expressed every thing by their dancing and gestures, without speaking. They wore a kind of wooden or iron sandals, called *scabilla*, which made a rattling noise when they danced.

The Romans had rope-dancers, who were often introduced in the time of the play. The plays were also often interrupted by the people calling out for various shows to be exhibited.

The actors were applauded or hissed, as

they performed their parts, or pleased or dis
pleased the spectators. Those actors who
were most approved received crowns.

The place where dramatic representations
were exhibited was called *theatrum,* a theatre.
In ancient times the people viewed the entertainments standing. A theatre, which was
being built A. U. 599, was by the appointment
of the senate ordered to be pulled down, as a
thing hurtful to good morals. Afterwards
temporary theatres were occasionally erected.
The most splendid was that of M. Æmilius
Scaurus, when ædile, which contained 80,000
persons, and was adorned with amazing magnificence and at an incredible expense. Pompey reared a theatre of hewn stone which
contained 40,000 persons ; but that he might
not incur the animadversion of the censors,
he dedicated it as a temple to Venus.

Theatres at first were open at the top, and
in excessive heat or rain, coverings were
drawn over them : but in later times they were
roofed.

The theatre was of an oblong semi-circular
form, like the half of an amphitheatre. The
benches, or seats, rose one above another, and
were distributed to the different orders as in
the amphitheatre. The foremost rows next
the stage, called *orchestra,* were assigned to
senators and ambassadors ; fourteen rows behind them to the *Equites ;* and the rest to the
people. The whole was called *cavea.*

The parts of the theatre allotted to the performers were called *scena, postscenium, proscenium, pulpitum,* and *orchestra.*

1. *Scena,* the scene, was adorned with columns, statues, and pictures of various kinds, according to the nature of the plays exhibited The scenery was concealed by a curtain, which contrary to the modern custom, was dropped or drawn down when the play began, and raised or drawn up when the play was over.

2. *Postscenium,* the place behind the scene where the actors changed their dress, and where those things were supposed to be done, which could not with propriety be exhibited on the stage.

3. *Proscenium,* the place before the scene, where the actors appeared. The place where the actors recited their parts was called *pulpitum ;* and the place where they danced, *orchestra,* which was about five feet lower than the *pulpitum.*

CHAPTER VI.

DOMESTIC AFFAIRS OF THE ROMANS.

SECTION I.

Dwellings, Furniture, &c.

THE houses of the Romans are supposed at first to have been simple cottages, thatched with straw. After the city was burnt by the Gauls it was rebuilt in a more solid and commodious manner, but the haste in building, prevented attention to the regularity of the streets.

In the time of Nero, the city was set on fire, and more than two thirds of it burnt to the ground. Nero himself was thought to have been the author of this conflagration. He beheld it from the tower of Mæcenas, and being delighted, as he said, with the beauty of the flame, played the taking of Troy, dressed like an actor.

The city was rebuilt with greater regularity and splendor. The streets were made straight and broader. The areas of the houses were measured out, and their height restricted to seventy feet. Each house had a portico before it fronting the street, and did not communicate with any other by a common wall as formerly.

Buildings in which several families lived were called *insula;* houses in which one family lived, *domus.*

The *vestibulum* was not properly a part of the house, but an empty space or court before the gate, through which was an access to it. The vestibule of the golden palace of Nero was so large, that it contained three porticoes a mile long each, and a pond.

The *janua* was the gate, generally raised above the ground so as to ascend it by steps. The gate or door was always opened inward, unless it was granted to any one by a special law to open his door to the street. A slave watched at the gate as porter, (*janitor,*) usually in chains, armed with a staff or rod, and attended by a dog.

The *atrium,* or hall, was of the form of an oblong square, surrounded with covered or arched galleries. Three sides of the *atrium* were supported on pillars. The side opposite to the gate was called *tablinum,* and the other two sides *alæ.*

In the atrium, the family were accustomed to sup. There also the nobility placed the images of their ancestors, and clients waited on their patrons. A hearth (*focus*) was here, on which was a fire kept always burning, near the gate, under the charge of the janitor; around it the images of the *lares* were placed.

The ancients had no chimneys, and were much annoyed with smoke.

The apartments of a house were variously constructed and arranged at different times, according to the different taste of individuals.

The Roman houses were covered with tiles of considerable breadth. The ancient Romans had only openings (*foramina*) in the walls to admit the light. Windows, (*fenestræ*,) under the emperors, were made of a certain transparent stone, (*lapis specularis*,) which could be split into thin leaves. Paper, linen cloth, and horn, seem likewise to have been used for windows. Glass windows are not mentioned till about the middle of the fourth century of the Christian era.

The magnificence of the Romans was greatly conspicuous in their country villas. A *villa* originally denoted a farm-house; but when increased wealth inspired the citizens with a taste for new pleasures, the *villa* became the abode of opulence and luxury.

A villa of this kind was divided into three parts, *urbana*, *rustica*, and *fructuaria*. The first contained dining-rooms, parlors, bed-chambers, tennis-courts, walks, terraces, &c.; the second contained accommodations for the various tribes of slaves and workmen, stables, &c.; and the third, wine and oil-cellars, corn-yards, barns, granaries, &c. In every villa there was commonly a tower, a large park for deer and wild beasts, and fish-ponds.

The Romans were uncommonly fond of gardens, stored with fruit and shady trees, adorned with beautiful statues, and joined by beautiful and shady walks.

The furniture of the Roman houses, which was at first very simple, changed with the general luxury. The eating-rooms were remārkable for their costly embellishments. The tables were originally square, made of wood, and on four feet; but the form was afterwards changed to circular or oval, supported on a single carved pedestal, and were richly inlaid with ivory, gold, and silver, and sometimes with precious stones. We read of a single table, formed of a kind of wood called citron wood, that cost more than eight thousand pounds sterling, (more than $35,000.)

In their rooms the Romans used portable furnaces, so that chimneys were not required as much as in modern times.

Section II.

Dress of the Romans.

The distinguishing part of the Roman dress was the *toga*, or gown; whence the Romans were called *gens togata*. The *toga* was

a loose, flowing, woollen robe, which covered
the whole body; round and close at the bottom, but open at the top down to the girdle;
without sleeves, so that the right arm was at
liberty; and the left supported a part of the
toga which was drawn up and thrown back
over the left shoulder, and thus formed what
was called *sinus*, a fold or cavity upon the
breast, in which things might be carried, or
with which the face and head might be
covered.

The *toga* in later times had several folds,
but anciently few or none. These folds, when
collected in a knot or centre, were called *umbo*.

When a person was engaged at any manual
labor, he tucked up his *toga* and girded it round
him.

The *toga* of the rich and noble was finer
and larger than that of the less wealthy. A
new *toga* was called *pexa;* when old and
threadbare, *trita.* The Romans were at great
pains to adjust the *toga* so that it might hang
gracefully.

The *toga* at first was worn by women as
well as men. But afterwards matrons wore a
different robe, (*stola*,) with a broad border or
fringe (*instita*) reaching to the feet; and also
when they went abroad, a loose outer robe,
thrown over the *stola* as a mantle or cloak,
called *palla.*

None but Roman citizens were permitted to
wear the toga, and banished persons were pro

hibited the use of it. Hence the *toga* is put for the dignity of a Roman.

The color of the *toga* was white, and candidates for office wore one more than usually white, (*toga candida.*) The *toga* in mourning was of a black or dark color, (*toga pulla.*) The mourning robe of women was called *ricinium.*

At entertainments the more wealthy Romans laid aside the *toga* and put on a particular robe called *synthesis.* Magistrates and certain priests wore a *toga*, bordered with purple, (*toga prætexta ;*) and young men, till they were seventeen years of age, and young women, till they were married, also wore a gown bordered with purple, (*toga prætexta.*) Generals at their triumphs wore an embroidered *toga*, (*toga picta.*)

Young men when they had completed the seventeenth year of their age, laid aside the *toga prætexta*, and assumed the manly gown, (*toga virilis.*) The ceremony of changing the *toga* was performed with great solemnity before the images of their ancestors, (*Lares.*)

The ancient Romans had no other clothing but the *toga*, but afterwards they wore under the toga a white woollen vest called *tunica*, which came down a little below the knees before, and the middle of the legs behind, at first without sleeves. Tunics with sleeves, or reaching to the ankles, were considered effeminate. The tunic was fastened by a girdle or belt (*cingulum*) about the waist, to keep it tight, which also served as a purse in which they kept their money. The tunic was worn by women as well as men, but the tunic of the women always came down to their feet and covered their arms.

The senators had a broad stripe of purple (or rather two stripes) sewed on the breast of their tunic, called *latus clavus;* and the *Equites* a narrow strip, (*angustus clavus.*)

The poor people, who could not purchase a *toga,* wore only the tunic.

Under the tunic the Romans wore another woollen covering, next to the skin, like our shirt, called *indusium.* Linen clothes were not used until the time of the emperors.

In later ages the Romans wore above the *toga* a kind of great-coat, called *lacerna,* with a covering for the head and shoulders, called *cucullus.* They had another kind of great-coat or surtout resembling the *lacerna,* but shorter and straighter, called *penula.* The *sagum* was a military cloak.

The Romans wore neither stockings nor breeches, but sometimes they wrapped their legs with pieces of cloth, (*fasciæ.*)

They had various coverings for their feet, but chiefly of two kinds. The one (*calceus,* or shoe) covered the whole foot, and was tied above with a latchet or lace; the other (*solea*) was a slipper or sandal, and covered only the sole of the foot, and was fastened with leathern thongs or strings.

The shoes of the senators were of a black color, and came up to the middle of their legs. They had a golden or silver crescent (*C*) on the top of the foot.

The shoes of the women were generally white, sometimes red, scarlet, or purple, adorned with embroidery and pearls. Men's shoes were generally black. The shoes of the soldiers (*caligæ*) were generally shod with nails. The shoes of comedians were called *socci*; of the tragedians, *cothurni*.

The ancient Romans went with their head bare, except at sacred rites, games, and festivals. They, however, threw over their head the lappet of their gown.

The head-dress of the women was at first very simple. But when riches and luxury increased, a woman's toilet was called her world, (*mundus muliebris*.) They anointed their hair with the richest perfumes; curled it with hot irons, adorned it with gold, pearls, precious stones; with crowns of garlands, and chaplets of flowers, bound with fillets or ribands of various colors. Every woman of fashion had, at least, one female hair-dresser, (*ornatrix*.)

Women used various cosmetics and washes to improve their color. They used ear-rings (*inaures*) of pearl and of precious stones, and gemmed necklaces, (*monilia*,) armlets, (*armillæ*,) and rings (*annuli*) of gold set with precious stones. Rings were used chiefly for seal-ing letters and papers, and were worn by men as well as women.

SECTION III.

Marriage Customs and Divorce.

A legal marriage among the Romans was made in three different ways, called *usus, confarreatio,* and *coemptio.*

1. *Usus* was when a woman, with the consent of her parents or guardians, lived with a man for a whole year without being absent three nights, and thus became his lawful wife. If absent three nights she was said to have interrupted the *usus,* and thus prevented a marriage.

2. *Confarreatio* was when a man and woman were joined in marriage by the *Pontifex Maximus,* or *Flamen Dialis,* in presence of at least ten witnesses, by a set form of words, and by tasting a cake made of salt, water, and flour, (*far.*) This was the most solemn form of marriage, and could only be dissolved by another kind of sacrifice called *diffarreatio.*

3. *Coemptio* was a kind of mutual purchase, when a man and woman were married by delivering to one another a small piece of money, and repeating certain words. The man asked the woman if she was willing to be the mis-

tress of his family. She answered, that she was willing. In the same manner the woman asked the man, and he made a similar answer.

The effects of this rite and of *confarreatio* were the same. The woman became a partner of all the substance and sacred rites of her husband, and if he died intestate and childless, she inherited his whole fortune ; and if he left children, she had an equal share with them. She assumed her husband's name together with her own. She resigned to him all her possessions, and acknowledged him as her lord and master, (*dominus.*) The goods which a woman brought to her husband besides her portion, were called *parapherna*, or *paraphernalia*. In the early days of the republic, dowries were very small, but afterwards the usual portion of a lady of senatorian rank was about 36,491 dollars.

Polygamy, or plurality of wives, was forbidden among the Romans.

The age of puberty or marriage was from fourteen for males, and twelve for girls. No young man or woman could marry without the consent of the parents or guardians.

On the wedding day, the bride was dressed in a long white robe, bordered with a purple fringe, or embroidered ribands, bound with a girdle or zone of wool tied in a knot, which the husband alone was to untie ; her face was covered with a red veil, to denote her modesty ; her hair was divided into six locks with the

N

point of a spear, and crowned with flowers;
her shoes were of the same color with her
veil, i. e. red or flame-colored.

No marriage was celebrated without consulting the auspices, and offering sacrifices to
the gods, especially to Juno, the goddess of
marriage.   Anciently, a hog was sacrificed.
The gall of the victim was always taken out,
and thrown away, to signify the removal of all
bitterness from marriage.   The marriage ceremony was performed in the house of the bride's
father or nearest relation.   In the evening, the
bride was conducted to her husband's house.
She was taken apparently by force from the
arms of her mother or nearest relation, in
memory of the violence used to the Sabine
women; and also to denote the reluctance
which she was supposed to feel at leaving the
paternal roof.   Three boys, whose parents
were alive, attended her; two of them sup-
porting her by the arm, and the third bearing
a flambeau of pine, or thorn (*tæda pinea*, or
spinea) before her.   There were five other
torches carried before her.   Maid-servants followed with a distaff, a spindle, and wool; intimating that she was to labor at spinning, as
the Roman matrons of old did.

A great number of relations and friends attended the nuptial procession, which was call
ed *officium*.

The door and door-posts of the bridegroom's
house were adorned with leaves and flowers,

and the rooms with tapestry.   When the bride came there, being asked who she was, she always answered, " *ubi tu Caius, ibi ego Caia,*" " where thou art Caius, there I shall be Caia," intimating that she would imitate the excellent housewife Caia, the wife of Tarquinius Priscus.   She then bound the door-posts with woollen fillets, and anointed them with the fat of swine or wolves, to avert fascination and enchantments, whence the name *uxor*, i. e. *unxor*, an anointer.   She was lifted over the threshold, or gently stepped over; for it was thought ominous to touch it with her feet, because the threshold was sacred to Vesta, the goddess of virgins.

Upon her entry the keys of the house were delivered to her, to denote her being intrusted with the management of the family.   A sheep's skin was spread before her, intimating that she was to work at the spinning of wool. Both she and her husband touched fire and water, because all things were supposed to be produced from these two elements, and with the water they bathed their feet.

The husband gave a feast to his relations and friends, and to those of the bride and her attendants, called *cœna nuptialis.*   Musicians sang the nuptial song, (*epithalamium.*)   Nuptial songs were sung by young women before the door of the nuptial chamber till midnight.   The husband scattered nuts among the boys, intimating that he dropped boyish amusements, and thenceforth was to act as a man. Young women when they were married consecrated their playthings and dolls (*pupæ*) to Venus. The guests were dismissed with small presents.

Next day another entertainment was given by the husband, called *repotia,* when presents were sent to the bride ; and she began to act as mistress of the family, by performing sacred rites.

A woman after marriage retained her former name.

Divorce, (*divortium,*) or a right to dissolve the marriage contract, was by the law of Romulus permitted to the husband but not to the wife ; not, however, without a just cause. A groundless or unjust divorce was punished with the loss of effects ; of which one half fell to the wife, and the other was consecrated to Ceres.

A man might then divorce his wife, if she had violated the conjugal faith, or had destroyed his offspring by poison, or brought upon him supposititious children ; if she had counterfeited his private keys, or even drunk wine without his knowledge.

Although the law allowed husbands this liberty of divorce, yet there is no instance of its being exercised for about 520 years. After this time divorces became common, not only for important reasons, but often on the most frivolous pretexts. If a wife was guilty of infidelity to her husband, she forfeited her dowry, but if the divorce was made without any fault of hers, the dowry was restored to her.

In the later times of the republic, the same liberty of divorce was exercised by the women as by the men.

Education of Children.

The education of the Romans at first corresponded with their rude state of society, and simple manner of life. But after their intercourse with the Greeks a more liberal plan of education was adopted. Public schools were opened for the reception of youth of both sexes.

The system of education among the Romans, about the time of Cicero, was much to be admired. The utmost attention was bestowed on the early formation of the mind and character.

The Roman matrons themselves nursed their children. The greatest attention was given to the language of the children. The attainment of a pure and correct expression was a great object; for the honors of the republic were the prize of eloquence.

In literature and the accomplishments of polished life, they were alike instructed.

From the earliest dawn of reason, a course

of discipline was pursued by some matron of the family; and as the children grew to manhood they were habituated to all the various athletic exercises that could impart agility or grace, and fit them for the profession of arms. At the age of seventeen years, young men assumed the manly robe; (*toga virilis ;*) and at this time, young men of rank were placed under the protection of some senator or eminent orator, whom they were to study to imitate, and under whose auspices they were initiated into public business.

Eloquence and the military art were the surest roads to preferment. These accordingly were made high objects of pursuit with the Roman youth. Eloquence (*eloquentia* or *facundia*) was taught as a science at public schools.

Boys of rank were attended to school by a slave, called *capsarius* or *librarius*, who carried their books, writing materials, &c. A private instructor was called *pædagogus ;* a public teacher, *præceptor*, *magister*, or *doctor*.

Boys of inferior rank carried their satchels and books themselves.

From the care which the Romans bestowed upon the education of their youth, both male and female, arose the large number of great men and eminent women which Rome produced, and the virtues with which they were adorned, during the brilliant era of the republic.

Roman literature, in the Augustan era, was but little inferior to that of the Greeks.

SECTION V.

Manners and Customs in Private Life. Entertainments, &c.

The food of the ancient Romans was of the simplest kind, principally vegetables; and wine was scarcely known among them. Their chief magistrates, when not occupied in the duties of their office, cultivated the ground with their own hands; sat down at the same board, and partook of the same food with their servants. But when riches were introduced, by the extension of conquest, the manners of the people were changed, and luxury seized all ranks. The pleasures of the table became the great object of attention.

The principal meal of the Romans was called *cœna*, supper. The usual time for this was the ninth hour, or three o'clock, P. M., in summer, and the tenth hour in winter. It was esteemed luxurious to sup more early.

About noon the Romans took a meal called *prandium*, dinner; which anciently was called *cœna*. In this meal they usually took only a little light food.

Besides the *cœna* and *prandium*, it became customary to take in the morning a breakfast, (*jentaculum;*) and some delicacy after supper to eat with their drink, called *Commissatio.*

At first they sat at meals. The custom of

reclining on couches, (*lecti* or *tori*,) was introduced from the eastern nations; and at first
adopted only by the men, but afterwards allowed also to the women. The images of the
gods used to be placed in this posture in a *lectisternium*. Boys and young men, below seventeen years of age, sat at the foot of the
couch of their parents and friends.

The custom of reclining took place only at
supper. There was no formality at other
meals. Persons took them alone, or in company, standing or sitting.

On each couch there were commonly three
persons. They lay with the upper part of the
body reclined on the left arm, the head a little raised, the back supported by cushions, and
the limbs stretched out at full length, the feet
of the first behind the back of the second, and
his feet behind the back of the third, with a
pillow between each. In conversation, those
who spoke raised themselves almost upright,
supported by cushions. When they ate, they
raised themselves on their elbow, and made
use of the right hand; and sometimes of both
hands. We do not read of their using any
knives or forks.

The tables (*mensæ*) of the Romans were anciently square, and called *cibilæ*, on three sides
of which were placed three couches; the
fourth side was left empty for the slaves to
bring in and take out the dishes. When the
semicircular couch (*sigma*) was introduced,

tables were made round. The tables were usually brought in and out with the dishes on them. Before the guests began to eat, they always washed their hands, and a towel (*mantile*) was furnished to wipe them. But each guest generally brought with him from home a table-napkin, (*mappa.*)

In later times, the Romans before supper were accustomed to bathe. The wealthy had baths, both cold and hot, at their own houses. There were public baths (*balinea*) for the use of the citizens at large, in which were separate apartments for the men and women. The usual time of bathing was two o'clock in summer, and three in winter.

The Romans before bathing took various kinds of exercise, as the ball, or tennis, (*pilæ ;*) throwing the javelin, and the *discus* or quoit ; rolling or throwing a bullet of stone, lead, or iron; riding, running, leaping, &c. Those who could not join in the exercise, took the air on foot, in a carriage, or a litter.

There were various places for walking, (*ambulacra,*) both public and private ; in the open air, and under covering. Covered walks, (*porticus,*) porticoes, were built in different places, chiefly around the *Campus Martius* and *Forum ;* supported by marble pillars, and adorned with statues and columns.

After bathing, they dressed for supper. They put on the *synthesis,* and slippers, which, when a person supped from home, were carried

O

to the place by a slave.   At feasts the guests
were crowned with garlands of flowers; and
their hair was perfumed with various oint-
ments.

They began their feasts by prayers and libations to the gods.   They never tasted any
thing without consecrating it.   They usually
threw a part into the fire as an offering to the
Lares, and when they drank, they poured out
a part, as a libation to some god on the table.
The table was held as sacred as an altar.   It
was consecrated by setting on it the images
of the *Lares*, and salt-cellars ; and particularly
the family salt-cellar, which was kept with
great care.

Salt was held in religious veneration by
the ancients, and was always used in sacrifices.

As the ancients had not proper inns for the
accommodation of travellers, the Romans when
they were in foreign countries, or at a distance
from home, were accustomed to lodge at the
houses of certain persons, whom they in return entertained at their houses in Rome. This
was esteemed a very intimate connection, and
called *hospitium.*

The supper (*cæna*) of the Romans usually
consisted of two parts, called *mensa prima*, the
first course, composed of various kinds of meat ;
and *mensa secunda* or *altera*, the second course,
consisting of fruits and sweetmeats.   They
usually began their entertainments with eggs

and ended with fruits.* In the time of supper, the guests were entertained with music and dancing, sometimes with pantomimes and actors; but the more sober had only persons to read select passages from books. Their highest pleasure at an entertainment arose from an agreeable conversation.

Wine was at first very rarely used as a beverage. Its chief use was in the worship of gods. Young men below thirty, and women all their life, were forbidden to drink it, unless at sacrifices. But afterwards these restrictions were removed, and wine mixed with water was a common drink at entertainments; and too often to a shameful excess. During the intervals of drinking, they often played at dice, (*alea.*)

The repasts were ended in the same manner as they began, by libations and prayers. The guests drank to the health of their host, and the master of the house gave them certain presents at their departure.

* Hence the phrase " *ab ovo, usque ad mala*," from the egg to the fruits, i. e. from the beginning to the end of supper.

Section VI.

Occupations, Arts, and Sciences.

The ancient Romans were so devoted to agriculture, that their most illustrious commanders were sometimes called from the plough. The senators commonly resided in the country, and cultivated the ground with their own hands. To be a good husbandman (*bonus colonus*, or *agricola*) was accounted the highest praise ; and whoever neglected his ground, or cultivated it improperly, was liable to the animadversion of the censors.

When riches increased, and the estates of individuals were enlarged, opulent proprietors let parts of their ground to other citizens, who paid a certain rent for them as our farmers or tenants, and were properly called *coloni*.

The grain chiefly cultivated by the Romans was wheat of different kinds, and called by different names, as *triticum, siligo, robus, far,* &c. Barley (*hordeum*) was cultivated, but not so extensively as wheat. It was the food of horses and sometimes of men. Oats (*avena*) were cultivated in like manner.

Trades and manufactures were considered among the Romans as degrading employments, and hence none but the lowest classes of the common people, and slaves, were engaged in hem. On this account there was always a very great multitude of idlers, who subsisted on the public bounty rather than labor at these occupations.

The ancient Romans used every method to encourage domestic industry in women. Spinning and weaving constituted their chief employment. But in after times women of rank and fortune became so luxurious that they thought this employment below them.

The fine arts were unknown at Rome until their victorious generals brought various specimens from the places which they conquered. They admired and imitated the master-pieces of Greece. But in execution they fell short of their models. By help derived from Grecian genius they have, however, left us many wonderful specimens in the arts, particularly in architecture.

The general literature of the Romans in their most intellectual era, was scarcely inferior to that of the Greeks. Poetry, history, oratory, philosophy, and the various styles of writing, were cultivated with great success.

In some instances splendid libraries were attached to the galleries of some affluent patricians, who patronized learning. These libraries were open to the inspection of the learned and curious, and contributed greatly to the advancement of knowledge at Rome.

The art of printing being unknown, books were sometimes written on parchment, but more generally on paper made from the leaves of a plant called *papyrus*, which grew and was prepared in Egypt. This plant was about ten cubits high, and had several coats, or skins, one above another, which they separated with a needle.

The instrument used in writing was a reed, sharpened and split at the point like our pens, and called *calamus*. Their ink was usually made from a black liquid emitted by the cuttle-fish.

The Romans commonly wrote only on one side of the paper, and joined one sheet to the end of the other till they finished what they had to write, and then rolled it on a cylinder or staff, hence called *volumen*, a volume.

But unimportant matters were generally written on tablets spread with wax. The writing was done by means of a metal pencil, called *stylus*, pointed at one end to scratch the letters, and flat at the other to smooth the wax when correction was necessary. As the Romans were not permitted to wear a sword or dagger in the city, they often upon a sudden provocation used the *stylus* as a weapon.

In writing letters the Romans always put their own name first, and then that of the person to whom they wrote. They always annexed the letter S for *salutem*, i. e. wishes health. They ended with *vale*, farewell. They never *sub*scribed their name, as is done in modern times.

Section VII.

Treatment of the Dead—Funeral Rites, &c.

The Romans paid the greatest attention to funeral rites, because they were of opinion that the souls of the unburied were not admitted into the abodes of the dead; or at least wandered a hundred years along the river Styx before they were allowed to cross it; for which reason, if the body of their friends could not be found, they erected to them an empty tomb, (*tumulus inanis*, or *cenotaphium*,) at which they performed the usual solemnities; and if they happened to see a dead body, they always threw some earth upon it. Hence no kind of death was so formidable as death by shipwreck.

When any one was at the point of death, his nearest relation present endeavored to catch his last breath with his mouth; for they believed that the soul, or living principle, (*anima*,) then went out at the mouth. He then closed the eyes and mouth of the deceased, and those present called the deceased by name several times, at intervals, repeating *ave* or *vale*, farewell. The corpse was bathed and perfumed, and dressed in the richest robes which the deceased had worn when alive, and laid on a couch in the vestibule, with the feet outward, when a lamentation was made.

The couch was often decked with leaves and flowers. If the deceased had ever received a crown for his bravery, it was placed at his head. A small coin was always put into his mouth, which he was to give to Charon, the ferryman of hell, for ferrying him over the river Styx.

A branch of cypress was placed at the door of the deceased, to prevent the *pontifex maximus* from entering and thereby being polluted; for it was unlawful for him, not only to touch a dead body, but even to look at it.

The Romans at first interred their dead, but they soon adopted the custom of burning from the Greeks. This practice, however, did not become general till towards the end of the republic.

A public funeral was called *indictivum;* a private one, *tacitum;* and the funeral of those who died under age or in infancy was called *acerbum,* or *immaturum.*

When a public funeral was intended, the corpse was usually kept for seven or eight days, with a keeper set to watch it. When the funeral was private, the body was not kept so long.

On the day of the funeral the dead body was carried out with the feet foremost, on a couch covered with rich cloth, supported usually on the shoulders of the nearest relations of the deceased, or his heirs. Poor citizens and slaves were carried to the funeral pile in a plain bier or coffin, (*sandapila,*) commonly by four bearers called *vespillones.* The funeral couches were sometimes open and sometimes covered.

All funerals were anciently solemnized in the night-time with torches, that they might not fall in the way of magistrates and priests, who were supposed to be polluted by seeing a corpse, so that they could not perform sacred rites till they were purified by an expiatory sacrifice. But in later times public funerals (*funera*) were celebrated in the day-time with torches also.

The order of the procession was regulated and every one's place assigned him by a person called *designator,* attended by lictors dressed in black. First went musicians of various kinds, with wind instruments of a larger size and deeper tone than those used on ordinary occasions; then mourning women, who were hired to lament or sing the praises of the deceased. After them came players and buffoons, who danced and sung. One of them, called *archimimus,* supported the character of the deceased, imitating his former words and actions. Then followed the freed-men of the deceased with a cap on their head. Some masters at their death freed all their slaves, from the vanity of having their funeral procession attended by a numerous train of freedmen.

Before the corpse were carried the images

of the deceased and those of his ancestors.
If he had distinguished himself in war, the
crowns and rewards which he had received
for his valor were displayed, together with
the spoils and standards he had taken from the
enemy. Behind the corpse walked the relations of the deceased, his sons with their heads
veiled, and his daughters with their heads
bare, and their hair dishevelled, the magistrates without their badges, and the nobility
without their ornaments. The nearest relations tore their garments and covered their
hair with dust, or plucked it out. The women particularly beat their breasts, tore their
cheeks, pretending to yield to all the impulses
of extravagant grief.

At the funeral of an illustrious citizen, the
corpse was carried through the *forum*, when
the procession stopped and a funeral oration
(*laudatio*) was delivered in favor of the deceased from the *rostrum* by his son, or some
near relation or friend.

From the *forum* the corpse was carried to
the place of burying or burial without the city.
The Vestal Virgins, and a few illustrious men
only. were buried in the city.

If the body was buried, the sepulchre was
strewed with flowers ; and the mourners took
a last farewell of the remains of the deceased.

If the corpse was burned, a funeral pile
(*rogus* or *pyra*) was constructed, in the shape
of an altar, upon which the body was laid with

the couch, and his eyes forced open. The nearest relations kissed the body, and then set fire to the pile with a torch, turning away their faces to show that they did it with reluctance. They threw into the fire various perfumes, the clothes and ornaments of the deceased; in short, every thing that was supposed to have been agreeable to him when alive.

As the *manes* were supposed to be appeased with blood, various animals were slaughtered at the pile, and thrown into it.

Instances are recorded of persons who came to life again on the funeral pile after it was set on fire, but too late to be preserved; and others who, having revived before the pile was ignited, returned home on their feet.

When the pile was burned down, the fire was extinguished and the embers soaked with wine, and the bones were collected by the nearest relations. The ashes and bones, sprinkled with the richest perfumes, were put into an urn (*urna*) of earth, marble, brass, silver, or gold, according to the wealth or rank of every one. Sometimes a small vial full of tears was put into the urn.

The urn was solemnly deposited in the family sepulchre, (*sepulchrum, tumulus, monumentum.*)

When the remains of the deceased were laid in the tomb, those present were sprinkled by a priest with pure water, (*aqua lustralis.*)

from a branch of olive, or laurel, to purify them. The friends, as a further purification, when they returned home, after being sprinkled with water, stepped over a fire, which was called *suffitis.* The house was also purified.

On the ninth day after the funeral a sacrifice was performed called *novendiale,* with which these solemnities were concluded.

Oblations and sacrifices to the dead were afterwards made, both occasionally and at stated periods. A feast was commonly added, called *silicarnium.*

The Romans in mourning kept themselves at home, avoiding every entertainment and amusement, neither cutting their hair nor beard, clothed in black, laying aside every kind of ornament. Under the emperors, however, women wore white in mourning.

In a public mourning the magistrates laid aside their badge of office.

After the introduction of Christianity into the empire, the practice of burning the dead fell into disuse.

CHAPTER VII.

TIME, MEASURES, WEIGHTS, AND MONEY OF THE ROMANS.

Section I.

Division of Time.

Romulus is said to have divided the year into ten months, the first of which was called *Martius*, March, from Mars, his supposed father; the second, *Aprilis*, April, either from the Greek name of Venus (Αφροδιτη) or because then trees and flowers open (*aperio*) their buds; the third, *Maius*, May, from *Maia*, the mother of Mercury; the fourth, *Junius*, June, from the goddess *Juno*. The rest were named from their number, *Quintilis, Sextilis, September, October, November*, and *December*. *Quintilis* was afterwards called *Julius*, July, from Julius Cæsar; and *Sextilis* was called *Augustus*, August, from Augustus Cæsar.

Numa added two months to these ten, called *Januarius*, January, from *Janus*; and *Februarius*, February, because the people were then purified (*februabatur*) by an expiatory sacrifice (*februalia*) from the sins of the whole

year; for this was anciently the last month in
the year.

Numa, in imitation of the Greeks, divided
the year into twelve months, according to the
course of the moon, consisting in all of three
hundred and fifty-four days. He afterwards
added one day more to make the number odd,
which was thought the more fortunate. But
as ten days and some hours were still wanting
to make the lunar year correspond to the
course of the sun, he appointed that every
other year an extraordinary month called *Men-
sis Intercalaris* should be inserted between the
23d and 24th days of February. The interca-
lating of this month was left to the discretion
of the *pontifices*, who by inserting more or
fewer days made the current year longer or
shorter, as was most convenient for themselves
or friends. Julius Cæsar when he became
master of the state resolved to put an end to
this disorder, and abolishing this intercalary
month, he adjusted the year according to the
course of the sun, and assigned to each month
the number of days which they still contain.
To make matters proceed regularly henceforth,
he inserted in the current year, besides the intercalary month of twenty-three days, two extraordinary months between November and
December, the one of thirty-three the other
of thirty-four days; so that this year, which
was called the last year of *confusion*, consisted of sixteen months, or four hundred and

forty-five days.   After this, from the first of
the ensuing January, the number of months
was regular.   All this was effected by the
care and skill of Sosigenes, a celebrated as-
tronomer of Alexandria, whom Cæsar had
brought to Rome for that purpose A. U. 707.
This is the celebràted Julian, or solar year,
which continues in use to this day in all Christian countries.

The months were divided into three parts,
kalends, (*kalendæ,*) nones, (*nonæ,*) and ides,
(*idus.*)   The first day of the month was called
the *kalends,* the fifth day the *nones,* and the
thirteenth day the *ides;* except in March, May,
July, and October, when the *nones* fell on the
seventh, and the *ides* on the fifteenth.

The ancient Romans did not divide their
time into weeks as we do, in imitation of the
Jews.   The custom of dividing into weeks
(*hebdomades*) was introduced under the empe-
rors.   The days of the week were named
from the planets as they still are, *Dies Solis,*
Sunday ; *Dies Lunæ,* Monday ; *Dies Martis,*
Tuesday ; *Dies Mercurii,* Wednesday ; *Dies
Jovis,* Thursday ; *Dies Veneris,* Friday ; *Dies
Saturni,* Saturday.

The Romans, in marking the days of the
month, counted backward.   Thus they called
the last day of December, *Pridie Kalendas,*
that is, the day before the kalends of January ;
the day before that, or the thirtieth of December, they called *Tertio Kal. Jan.,* or the third

day before the kalends of January, and so on, to the thirteenth, when came the ides of December. Thus the 14th day of April, June, September, and November, was marked XVIII *kal.* of the following month; the 15th, XVII *kal.*, &c.

In leap year, that is, when February has twenty-nine days, which happens every fourth year, both the 24th and 25th days of that month were marked *Sexti Kalendas Martii,* the sixth kalends of March, that is, the sixth day before the kalends of March; and hence this year was called *Bissextilis.*

The Romans counted *in* the day on which they dated, and called the *second* day before the kalends, Nones or Ides, the *third,* (*tertio,*) and so on. And as the kalends are not the last day of the current month, but the first of the month following, we must take this additional day into consideration in accommodating our calendar to their dates.

The Roman date of any given day of our months, may be found by the following method.

RULE. Add *one* to the number of the Nones and Ides, and *two* to the number of days in the month for the Kalends, then subtract the number of the day: *e. g.* to find the Roman date of the 21st of July: to 31, add 2=33; from this take 21, the given day of the month, and the remainder 12 is the Roman date 12, Kal. Aug., that is, the 12th day before the kalends of August.

A TABLE OF THE KALENDS, NONES, AND IDES

Days of one Month.	January, August, December.	March, May, July, October.	April, June, September, November.	February.
1	Kalendæ.	Kalendæ.	Kalendæ.	Kalendæ.
2	4 Nonas.	6 Nonas.	4 Nonas.	4 Nonas.
3	3 Nonas.	5 Nonas.	3 Nonas.	3 Nonas.
4	Pridie Nonas.	4 Nonas.	Pridie Nonas.	Prid.Nonas
5	Nonæ.	3 Nonas.	Nonæ.	Nonæ.
6	8 Idus.	Pridie Nonas.	8 Idus.	8 Idus.
7	7 Idus.	Nonæ.	7 Idus.	7 Idus.
8	6 Idus.	8 Idus.	6 Idus.	6 Idus.
9	5 Idus.	7 Idus.	5 Idus.	5 Idus.
10	4 Idus.	6 Idus.	4 Idus.	4 Idus.
11	3 Idus.	5 Idus.	3 Idus.	3 Idus.
12	Pridie Idus.	4 Idus.	Pridie Idus.	Prid. Idus.
13	Idus.	3 Idus.	Idus.	Idus.
14	19 Kalendas.	Pridie Idus.	18 Kalendas.	16 Kal.
15	18 Kalendas.	Idus.	17 Kal.	15 Kal.
16	17 Kalendas.	17 Kalendas.	16 Kal.	14 Kal.
17	16 Kalendas.	16 Kal.	15 Kal.	13 Kal.
18	15 Kalendas.	15 Kal.	14 Kal.	12 Kal.
19	14 Kalendas.	14 Kal.	13 Kal.	11 Kal.
20	13 Kalendas.	13 Kal.	12 Kal.	10 Kal.
21	12 Kalendas.	12 Kal.	11 Kal.	9 Kal.
22	11 Kalendas.	11 Kal.	10 Kal.	8 Kal.
23	10 Kalendas.	10 Kal.	9 Kal.	7 Kal.
24	9 Kalendas.	9 Kal	8 Kal.	6 Kal.
25	8 Kalendas.	8 Kal.	7 Kal.	5 Kal.
26	7 Kalendas.	7 Kal.	6 Kal.	4 Kal.
27	6 Kalendas.	6 Kal.	5 Kal.	3 Kal.
28	5 Kalendas.	5 Kal.	4 Kal.	Pridie Kal.
29	4 Kalendas.	4 Kal.	3 Kal.	
30	3 Kalendas.	3 Kal.	Pridie Kalendas.	
31	Pridie Kalendas.	Pridie Kalendas.		

The day among the Romans was either civil or natural. The civil day (*dies civilis*) was from midnight to midnight. The natural day (*dies naturalis*) was from the rising to the setting of the sun. It was divided into twelve hours, which of course were of different length at different seasons of the year. They measured time by dials, (*horologiæ solariæ;*) and

P

water time-pieces, (*clepsydræ,*) which discharged a certain quantity of water in certain times, and served by night as well as by day.

Section II.

Dry and Liquid Measures, and Measures of Length and Weights.

The measure of capacity most frequently mentioned by Roman authors is the *amphora*. This was a liquid measure of more than seven gallons, but .was sometimes used by writers with reference to no certain measure.

The Roman Dry Measures were, in English Corn Measure—

	Pecks.	Gals.	Pt.	Cub. Inch.
1 Ligula	0	0	0 1-48th	0
1 Cyathus, or 4 Ligulæ,............	0	0	0 1-12th	0 1-25th
1 Acetabulum, or 1 1-2 Cyathi,........	0	0	0 1-8th	0 3-50ths
1 Hemina, or 4 Acetabula,............	0	0	0 1-2	0 6-25ths
1 Sextarius, or 2 Heminæ, ...	0	0	1	0 12-25ths
1 Semi-Modius, or 2 Sextarii, ...	0	1	0	3 21-25ths
1 Modius, or 2 Semi-Modii, ...	1	0	0	7 17-25ths

The Roman Liquid Measures were, in English Wine Measure—

	Gals.	Pts.	Cub. Inch.
1 Ligula,............................	0	0 1-48th	0 3 25ths
1 Cyathus, or 4 Ligulæ, ...	0	0 1-12th	0 12-25ths
1 Acetabulum, or 1 1-2 Cyathi,........	0	0 1-8th	0 17-25ths
1 Quartarius, or 2 Acetabula, ...	0	0 1-4th	1 10-25ths
1 Hemina, or 2 Quartarii,............	0	0 1-2	2 20-25ths
1 Sextarius, or 2 Heminæ, ...	0	1	5 16-25ths
1 Congius, or 6 Sextarii,............	0	7	4 47-50ths
1 Urna, or 4 Congii,..................	3	4 1-2	5 1-3
1 Amphora, or 2 Urnæ,................	7	1	10 2-3ds
1 Culeus, or 20 Amphoræ, ...	143	3	11 19-200ths

The *quadrantal* is the same as the *amphora*
The *Cadus, Congiarius,* and *Dolium,*.denote no
certain measure, but merely a *cask* or *keg.*

The *Sextarius* was divided into twelve equal
parts called *cyathi,* and therefore the *calices*
were called *sextantes, quadrantes,* &c., according to the number of *cyathi* they contained.

The Roman Measures of Length reduced to
English were—

	Eng. paces.	Ft.	Inches
1 Digitus transversus, or *finger's breadth,*....	0	0	0 18-25ths
1 Uncia, or *thumb's breadth, or inch,* } .... or 1 1-3 Digiti, }	0	0	0 24-25ths
1 Palmus Minor, *or hand's breadth,* or 3 Unciæ,	0	0	2 45-50ths
1 Pes, or *foot,* or 4 Palmi,.....................	0	0	11 15-25ths
1 Palmipes, or 1 1-4 Pedes, ...	0	1	2 1-2
1 Cubitus, or 1 1-5 Palmipedes,..............	0	1	5 10-25ths
1 Gradus, or 1 2-5ths Cubiti,.................	0	2	5 1-100ths
1 Passus, or *pace,* or 2 Gradus,..................	0	4	10 1-50ths
1 Stadium, or *furlong,* or 125 Passus,.........	120	4	4 1-2
1 Milliare, or *mile,* or 8 Stadia, ...	967	0	0

The ancient Roman Land Measure was—

100 Square Roman feet equal		1 Scrupulum of land
4 Scrupula,	or 400 Roman feet square,	1 Sextulus
1 1-5th Sextuli,	or 480 " " "	1 Actus
6 Sextuli, or 5 Actus, or 2,400 " " "		1 Uncia of land
6 Unciæ,	or 14,400 " " "	1 Square Actus
2 Square Actus,	or 28,800 " " "	1 Jugerum or acre
3 Jugera, ...		1 Heredium
100 Heredia, ...		1 Centuria.

There was a measure called *clima,* equal to
3600 square feet.

The principal Roman weight was the *AS*
or *libra,* a pound, divided into twelve parts or
ounces, (*unciæ ;*) thus, *uncia,* 1-12th of an *as,*
or one ounce ; *sextans,* 1-6th ; *quadrans,* 1-4th ;
triens, 1-3d ; *quincunx,* 5-12ths ; *semis,* 1-2 ;
septunx, 7-12ths ; *bes* or *bessis,* 2-3ds ; *dodrans,*

3-4ths; *dextans* or *decunx,* 5-6ths; *deunx,* 11-12ths of an *as.*

The *Uncia* was also divided thus : *semuncia,* 1-2 of an *uncia* or ounce ; *duella,* 1-3d ; *sicilicus* 1-4th ; *sextula,* 1-6th ; *drachma,* 1-8th ; *hemisesela,* 1-12th ; *tremissis, scrupulus, scripulum,* 1-24th of an ounce.

As was applied to any thing divided into twelve parts, as to an acre, to liquid measure, to money, &c.

The pound (*libra*) was equal to 10 ounces, 18 pennyweights, 13 5-7ths grains of English *Troy* weight, or nearly 12 ounces *Avoirdupois*

Section III.

Money of the Romans.

The Romans, like other ancient nations, at first had no coined money, (*pecunia signata,*) but either exchanged commodities with one another, or used a certain weight of uncoined brass, (*æs rude,*) or other metal.

Servius Tullius first stamped pieces of brass with the image of cattle, oxen, swine, &c., (*pecudes,* whence the word *pecunia,* money.) Silver was first coined A. U. 484 ; and gold sixty-two years after. Silver money, however, seems to have been in use at Rome before that time, but of foreign coinage. The Roman coins were then only of brass.

The first brass coin (*nummus æris*) was called *as*, and was of a pound weight. The others were *semisses, trientes, quadrantes*, and *sextantes*. These coins at first had the full weight which their names imported.

In the first Punic war the *as* was coined weighing only one-sixth of a pound, or two ounces; in the second Punic war, it was made to weigh only one ounce; and afterwards, A. U. 563, half an ounce.

The sum of three *asses* was called *tressis*, of ten, *decussis*; of twenty, *vicessis*; and so on to a hundred, *centussis*.

The silver coins were—*Denarius*, the value of which was ten *asses*, marked with letter X.—*Quinarius*, five *asses*, marked V.—and Sestertius, two *asses* and a half, commonly marked by the letters L. L. S. for *libra libra semis*, or by abbreviation, H. S.; and often called *nummus*, because it was in most common use.

From every pound of silver were coined 100 *denarii*, so that at first, a pound of silver was equal in value to a thousand pounds of brass. But when the weight of the *as* was diminished, it bore the same proportion to the *denarius* as before, till it was reduced to one ounce, and then a *denarius* was valued at sixteen *asses*; a *quinarius*. for eight *asses*; and a *sestertius* for four; which proportion continued when the *as* was reduced to half an ounce. But the weight of silver money also varied under the emperors.

There were silver coins of less value ; *libella*, equivalent to an *as* or tenth part of a *denarius ; sembella*, worth half a pound of brass, or the twentieth part of a *denarius ;* and *teruncius*, the fortieth part of a *denarius.*

A golden coin was first struck at Rome in the second Punic war, A. U. 546, and was called *aureus ;* equal in weight to two *denarii* and a *quinarius*, and in value to twenty-five *denarii* or one hundred *sestertii.* The common rate of gold to silver during the republic was tenfold.

Money was coined in the temple of *Juno Moneta ;* whence our word money.

There are several Grecian coins mentioned by Roman writers, some of them equal to Roman coins and some not : *drachma*, equal to a *denarius ; mina*, equal to a Roman *libra · talentum*, equal to sixty *libræ ; tetradrachma*, equal to four denarii ; *obolus*, the sixth part of a *denarius.*

The Romans usually computed money by *sestertii* or *sestertia.* *Sestertius* is the name of a coin, and *sestertium* the name only of a sum. When a numeral adjective is joined with *sestertii* it means just so many sesterces ; thus, *decem sestertii*, ten sesterces ; but when it is joined with *sestertia*, it means so many thou sand sestertii; thus *decem sestertia,* ten thousand sesterces.

If a numeral adjective of another case is joined to the genitive plural, it denotes so many thousand, as, *decem sestertium,* ten thousand sesterces. If a numeral adverb is joined, it denotes so many hundred thousand, as *decies sestertium,* ten hundred thousand *sesterces.* If the numeral adverb stand by itself, the signification is the same.

When sums are marked by letters, if the letters have a line over them, they signify so many hundred thousand sesterces; thus H. S. M̅. C̅. denotes the sum of 1,100 times 100,000 sesterces, i. e. 110,000,000, whereas H. S. M. C. without the line over them, signifies only 1,100 sesterces.

When the numbers are distinguished by points, in two or three orders, the first towards the right hand signifies units; the second, thousands; and the third, hundred thousands; thus, III. XII. DC. HS. denotes 300,000; 12,000; and 600 H. S.; in all making 312,600 sesterces.

The Romans sometimes expressed sums by talents or pounds, (*talenta* or *libræ,*) but the common computation was by *sestertii* or *nummi.*

The Roman coins reduced to Federal money:

BRASS.

A Quadrans, or teruncius, is equal to			$0.00.35	of a cent.
A Triens,	-	-	-	0.00.47	"
A Semissis,	-	-	-	0.00.71	"
An As or æs,	-	-	-	0.01.43	"

SILVER.

A Teruncius,	-	-	-	0.00.35 of a cent
A Sembella,	-	-	-	0.00.71 "
A Libella,	-	-	-	0 01.43 "
A Sestertius, or Nummus,		-		0.03.57 "
A Quinarius,	-	-	-	0.07.17 "
A Denarius,	-	-	-	0.14.35 "

GOLD.

An Aureus,	-	-	-	3.58.79 of a cent

The interest of money was called *fœnus* or *usura ;* the capital or principal, *caput* or *sors.* When the interest at the end of the year was added to the principal, and likewise yielded interest, it was *anatocismus anniversarius*, compound interest.

The interest allowed by the laws of the twelve tables was only one per cent., but these and other regulations were eluded by the art of the usurers, and in the year A. U. 795, the interest was twelve per cent., though it fell, upon the death of Antony and Cleopatra, to four per cent.

The Romans usually paid money by the intervention of a banker, (*mensarius.*) The interest of money was commonly paid on the kalends.

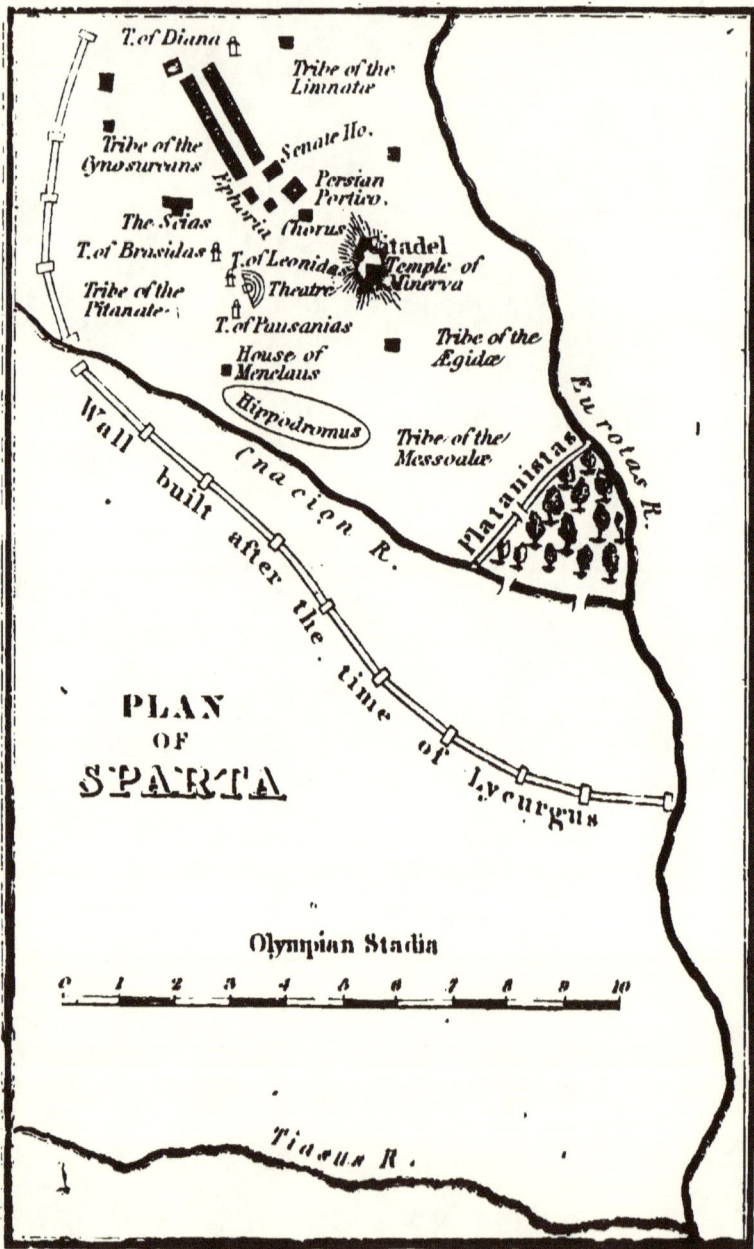

PLAN
OF
SPARTA

T. of Diana
Tribe of the Limnatæ
Tribe of the Cynosureans
Senate Ho.
Ephoria
Persian Portico
The Scias
Chorus
T. of Brasidas
T. of Leonidas
Citadel
Temple of Minerva
Tribe of the Pitanatæ
Theatre
T. of Pausanias
House of Menelaus
Tribe of the Ægidæ
Hippodromus
Tribe of the Messoalæ
Platanistas
Eurotas R.
Wall (nacion R. built after the time of Lycurgus

Olympian Stadia

0 1 2 3 4 5 6 7 8 9 10

Tiasus R.

ANTIQUITIES OF GREECE.

ANTIQUITIES OF GREECE

CHAPTER I.

GEOGRAPHY AND TOPOGRAPHY.

Section I.

A General Geographical View of Greece, in Boundaries and Principal Divisions.

The name of Hellas, which afterwards served to designate the whole of what we now call Greece, was originally applied only to a particular district of Thessaly. At that early period, as we are informed by Thucydides, the common appellation of Hellenes (Greeks) had not yet been received in that wide acceptation which was subsequently attached to it, but each separate district had its distinctive name, derived generally from the clan or tribe by which it was possessed, or from the chieftain who was regarded as the progenitor of their race.

It is difficult to say, with precision, what are the boundaries of ancient Greece. By some, Illyria, Macedonia, and Epirus, are excluded from its territory; while, by others, they are considered as forming a part of it. As these kingdoms, especially Macedonia, exerted a great influence upon the affairs of Greece, and participated in some measure in her counsels, we think it will be proper to include them in her boundaries.

Greece then may be considered as consisting of three general divisions:—the first or northern division; comprising, Epirus, Illyria, Macedonia, and Thrace;—the second or middle division, called Græcia Propria; comprehending Thessalia, Arcanania and its islands, Ætolia, Doris, Locris, Phocis, Bœotia, Attica, Megaris, and Eubœa;—the third, or southern division, called Peloponnesus; including Achaia, Corinthia, Argolis, Arcadia, Elis, Messenia, and Laconia, together with the adjacent islands.

Greece had for its northern boundary, the great chain of mountains which commences near the head of the Hadriatic sea, and terminates at the Euxine sea. This chain was nearly all included in what the ancients called *Hæmus Montes.* The eastern boundary was the Ægean sea, as also a small part of the Tuxine, and the straits which unite these two seas with the intervening Propontis, or modern sea of Marmora. On the south it was bounded by the Cretan or Candian sea, and on the west, by the Ionian and Hadriatic seas.

No part of Europe, if we except Switzerland, is so mountainous throughout the whole of its extent as Greece. The ruggedness of its surface, however, gave additional sublimity as well as beauty to its scenery. Its rivers, though so much celebrated by the poets, are only small streams. There are but few lakes in Greece.

SECTION II.

Athens.

The city of Athens, the capital of Attica, was founded by Cecrops, an Egyptian. At first it was called Cecropia, from the name of its founder; afterwards, Athens, (Ἀθῆναι,) in honor of the goddess Minerva, whom the Greeks called Ἀθήνη, and who received the privilege of giving the city a name in preference to Neptune. The Athenians thought themselves the most ancient nation of Greece, and supposed themselves the original inhabitants of Attica. Hence they called themselves αὐτόχθονες, " produced from the *same earth* which they inhabited;" γηγενεῖς, "sons of the earth;" and τέττιγες, "grasshoppers," because those insects were supposed to have sprung from the ground.

It was in the time of Pericles that Athens attained the summit of its beauty, property, and power. At this period, the whole of Athens, with its three ports, Piræus, Munychia, and Phalerum, connected by means of the celebrated long walls, formed one vast city within an enclosure of massive fortifications. The whole of this circumference was about . one hundred and seventy-four stadia, or twenty-two English miles. The number of gates belonging to ancient Athens is not known; but the existence of nine has been ascertained by classical writers.

The *Acropolis*, or *Cecropian citadel*, was situated on an elevated rock, which terminated abruptly in precipices on every side, except the western, whence alone it was accessible. On this side stood the *Propylæa* (portico or entrance) of the Acropolis. This was erected by Pericles, and intended as an entrance to the Parthenon, but was considered to rival that edifice in beauty and dimensions. It was of the most massy construction, and consisted of a great vestibule, with a front of six Doric columns. Beyond this vestibule was another supported by six pillars of the Ionic order: these formed the approach to the five gates or entrances of the citadel. The whole structure is said to have been five years in progress, and to have cost 2000 talents, equivalent to about 2,000,000 dollars.

The *Parthenon*, or temple of Minerva, was situated on the summit of the Acropolis, being far elevated above the Propylæa and adjacent edifices. In beauty and magnificence it far surpassed all other buildings of the kind, and was constructed entirely of Pentelic marble. The architect was Ictinus. It consisted of a cell surrounded with a peristyle, having eight Doric columns in the two fronts, and seventeen in the sides. The total elevation of the temple was sixty-five feet from the ground, its length two hundred and twenty-eight, and breadth one hundred and two feet. It was enriched within and without with matchless works of art executed by the first sculptors of Greece. The statue of Minerva was of ivory and gold, and was the noblest work of the renowned Phidias, if we except his statue of Jupiter Olympius, in Elis. This statue of Minerva was thirty-nine feet in height and clothed in a robe reaching to the feet. On the walls of the Parthenon were sculptured many battles in which the Athenians had been engaged.

On the southeast of the Acropolis stood the celebrated *Dionysiac theatre*, or theatre of Bacchus, in which were the statues of many of the tragic and comic writers. It was in this edifice that dramatic contests were decided. It was capable of containing thirty thousand

spectators. Near this was the *Odeum*, a mu-
sic-theatre, built by Pericles, and richly decorated with columns which terminated in a
point. On the northeast side of the Acropolis
was the *Prytaneum*, in which the laws of Solon were deposited. In this building were
several statues ; among others, that of Vesta,
before which a lamp was kept constantly
burning. Here the Presidents of the senate
(πρυτάνεις) resorted for the transaction of business. On the northwest of the Acropolis was
the *Areopagus*, or Hill of Mars, so called, according to some, because Mars had been cited
thither to trial for the murder of a son of Neptune. This celebrated court consisted of an
open space in which was an altar dedicated to
Minerva, and two rude seats of stone, for the
accused and his accuser. The *Pnyx* was
situated on rising ground opposite the Areopagus and near the walls of the city. In the
days of Athenian greatness, it was the usual
place of assembly for the people, especially
during elections. The celebrated *Bema*, from
which the orators addressed the people, was a
simple pulpit of stone. The *Museum* was another elevation in the same vicinity. It is said
to have received its name from the poet Mu-
sæus, who was interred there.

The old *Forum*, (Αγορα,) formed part of the
interior Ceramicus. It was very spacious,
and adorned with buildings dedicated to the
worship of the gods. It was here that public

assemblies of the people were held. But its chief use was for the resort of persons to buy and sell; and as every trade had different places assigned to it, the forum was divided into different parts, distinguished from each other by the names of the several articles exhibited for sale. One quarter was called Cyclus, (Κύκλος,) where slaves were bought, and also meat, fish, and other provisions. We also read of the women's market, (γυναικεία ἀγορά,) where they sold women's apparel;—of the fish-market, (ἰχθυόπωλις ἀγορά.) A particular stand was allotted to each vender, which he was not permitted to change. The time when goods were exposed for sale was called "full market," (πλήθουσα ἀγορά,) from the great number of persons assembled. To this place the inhabitants resorted every day to the average number of twenty thousand. The *Stoa Pœcile*, near the old forum, was so called from the celebrated paintings it contained, executed by the best artists. It was in this portico, (στοα,) that Zeno first opened his school. Hence his disciples were called Stoics. There were also many other porticoes (στοαί) in various parts of the city. North of the Areopagus was the celebrated *temple of Theseus*, erected in honor of this hero, after the battle of Marathon. It was esteemed by the Athenians in the highest reverence, and possessed an inviolable sanctuary. The interior was decorated with paintings, representing the achievements of Theseus.

Q

This noble structure, which has suffered but little from the injuries of time, has been converted into a Christian church. The *Olympeum* was one of the most ancient of the sacred edifices of Athens. Pisistratus raised a more magnificent structure on the site of the old building. Near the river Ilissus was the *Stadium*, erected for the celebration of games. It was a huge structure rising in the shape of an amphitheatre, and extended to the banks of the river. It was built of Pentelic marble, and was of such stupendous magnitude that Pausanias says it might be taken for a mountain on the banks of the Ilissus.

The *Pantheon* was a temple consecrated to *all the gods*, as its name indicates. It was a most magnificent structure, and was supported by one hundred and twenty columns of Phrygian marble. On the outside were engraven the histories of all the gods.

The *Ceramicus* was an extensive space of ground which contained many temples, theatres, porticoes, &c. It was divided into the outer and inner Ceramicus. The latter was full of public buildings, and was within the walls. The former was without the walls, and contained the tombs of the most illustrious warriors and statesmen of Athens. The road was lined as far as the Academy, on each side, with sepulchres of the gallant Athenians who had fallen in battle. At the termination of this burying ground was the *Academy*. It was surrounded with a wall, and adorned with groves, walks, and fountains, as well as statues and altars to many of the gods. Here Plato first opened his school. Without the enclosure a monument was erected to his memory.

The *Cynosarges* was a space of ground consecrated to Hercules, and contained a gymnasium, and groves frequented by philosophers.

The *Lyceum* was a sacred enclosure dedicated to Apollo, near the river Ilissus. It was adorned with fountains, groves, and buildings, and was the usual place of exercise for the Athenian youths who devoted themselves to military pursuits. It was also frequented by philosophers, and those fond of retirement and study. It was especially the favorite walk of Aristotle and his disciples, who thence obtained the name of Peripatetics.* The Lyceum, the Academy, and the Cynosarges were the three principal gymnasia, appropriated to the education of youth.

The *Gymnasia* of the Greeks were not single edifices, but a number of buildings united, so capacious as to contain several thousand persons. They were erected and maintained at the public expense, for the use of philosophers, rhetoricians, &c., and for pugilists, wrestlers, and others, who might exercise themselves at the same time without suffering any inter-

---

* From περὶ and πατέω, to walk about.

ruption. They consisted principally of the following divisions :—1. Στοαί, 'porticoes,' which were filled with ἐξέδραι, 'apartments,' furnished with seats, and fitted for study and discourse. 2. 'Εφήβεια, 'play-grounds,' where the ἐφήβοι, or youths exercised. 3. 'Αποδυτήρια γυμναστήρια, 'undressing rooms.' 4. Παλαιστρα, 'the palæstra,' or places for wrestling, the floors of which were covered with dust or gravel to prevent the combatants from slipping. 5. Θερμαι, λουτρά, 'hot' and ' cold baths.' 6. Στάδια, 'the stadia,' large semicircles in which exercises were performed.

The *Long Walls*, which connected Athens with its several ports, were first planned and commenced by Themistocles after the Persian war. One of these walls was called the Piraic, and sometimes the ' northern wall ;' the other, Phileric, or ' southern wall.' The length of the northern wall was about four and a half miles, and of the southern, nearly four miles. The height of each was sixty feet. Phalerum, before the time of Themistocles, had been the usual port for ships. But that great statesman perceived the superior advantages that the Piræus offered, and accordingly it was fitted up. It was the principal naval station, and was very commodious, containing three smaller harbors. It was well covered with buildings, forums, stoæ, storehouses, &c. The port of Munychia was an important position on account of the security it afforded to the maritime dependencies of Athens, and was always well fortified. Phalerum was the most ancient of the three harbors, but after the erection of the docks (ὅρμοι) in the Piræus, it ceased to be of any importance in a maritime view.

There were two rivers which supplied Athens with water, the principal one of which was the Ilissus, on the east side of the city. The other, the Cephissus, was smaller, and on the western side, it ran under the long walls.

The two principal mountains were the Anchesmus and Hymettus. The former was not very elevated, and had a statue of Jupiter upon its summit. Hymettus is more celebrated. It was famous for its fragrant flowers, and excellent honey. It produced good marble, and, according to some, contained silver mines.

Section III.

Sparta or Lacedæmon.

Sparta was situated a little north of the centre of Laconia, on the west bank of the Eurotas. During the most flourishing period of the Spartan history, it contained but few public buildings, and those were not noted either for their size or their architectural beauty. It continued without walls during this same period, Lycurgus having inspired his

countrymen with the idea, that the real de
fence of a town consisted chiefly in the valor
of its citizens. When Sparta became subject
to despotic rulers, fortifications were erected,
which rendered the town capable of sustain-
ing a regular siege. It was then about six
miles in circumference. It was encompassed
with vineyards, olive or plane trees, gardens,
and summer houses. The city was composed
of five villages, which were separated from
each other by intervals of different extent, and
each of which was occupied by one of the five
tribes of Sparta.

The *Forum* was situated towards the northern part of the city, and contained the Senate-
House, and the *Halls* of the *Ephori*, *Nomophy-
laces*, and *Bidiœi*.* The *Persian Portico* was
in this part of the city, and was so called from
its having been erected from the spoils taken
from that people. The *Chorus* was that part
of the Forum in which dances were performed
in honor of Apollo during the gymnastic games
of the youth. Near this stood the temples of
Tellus and *Jupiter*. North of these was the
temple of *Diana*. The *Scias* was a building
where the assemblies of the people were held.
On the south of the Forum were the *Cenotaph*
of *Brasidas*, (a Lacedæmonian general,) and
a Theatre of white marble ; and opposite to it
were the *Tombs* of *Pausanias* and *Leonidas*.
Orations were here annually recited, and games

* See Chap. III, Sec. II

celebrated, in which none but Spartans were admitted to contend for prizes. The names of those who fought in the battles against the Persians, at Thermopylæ, were inscribed on a pillar near the monument. South of the Theatre was the *Dromus*, or race-course of the Spartan youths, which contained two gymnasia.

Sparta did not possess a citadel noted for its elevation; but as there were several hills without the city, the highest of them was called the *Acropolis.* Here was the temple of *Minerva.* This edifice was decorated with elegant specimens of sculpture in brass, representing the labors of Hercules, the exploits of the Tyndaridæ, of Perseus, and the birth of Minerva.

Of all the Grecians, the Spartans lived in the most plain and simple manner. Their houses were free from ornament, though of great solidity; and the monuments which they erected to their heroes, were by no means expensive or magnificent.

CHAPTER II.

CIVIL GOVERNMENT AND POLITICAL ECONOMY OF ATHENS.

Section I.

Inhabitants of Athens.

Tne inhabitants of Athens were divided into three ranks or classes:—1. *citizens,* (πολῖται;) —2. *resident foreigners,* (μέτοικοι;)—3. *servants* or *slaves,* (δοῦλοι.) The number of the inhabitants has been variously estimated. In the census taken by Demetrius Phalerius, in the year 314 B. C., the number amounted to 21,000 citizens; 10,000 foreigners, and 40,000 slaves. In its highest prosperity Athens probably contained about 80,000 citizens, from 20,000 to 40,000 foreigners, and 400,000 slaves.

A citizen could only be such by birth or adoption. To be a natural denizen of Athens it was necessary to be born of Athenian parents, both free. The people could confer the freedom of the city upon strangers; and those who were so adopted, enjoyed most of the rights and privileges of natural citizens. The citizens alone enjoyed the privileges of being present at all public assemblies, and of sharing in the government of the state. When the young men had attained the age of twenty, they were enrolled upon the list of citizens, after having taken a solemn oath; and it was in virtue of that public and solemn act that they became members of the state.

Solon divided the citizens into four classes, according to their rank and fortune:—1. The πενταχοσιομέδιμνοι, 'five-hundred-measure-men,' or those who had an annual income of five hundred measures;—2. The ἱππεῖς, 'knights,' those who could furnish a horse equipped, or were worth three hundred medimni or measures, (about four hundred and thirty-one bushels;) —3. The ζευγῖται, 'zeugitæ,' who were worth one hundred and fifty measures;—4. The Ͽῆτες, 'menials,' the lowest class of the people, who were not eligible to any office under government.

The second class of the inhabitants were the μέτοικοι, 'sojourners,' 'foreigners,' residing in the city. They had no share in the government, nor votes in the public assemblies, and could not be admitted to any public office. They were obliged to submit to any enactment the citizens might choose to pass against them. They were, however, permitted to place themselves under the protection of some citizen, who acted as their patron, (προστάτης,) and to whom they were obliged, in turn, to render certain duties and services. If they

R

failed in performing what was required, their property was confiscated. The head of every family was obliged to pay into the public treasury the sum of twelve drachms for himself, and six for his children. In default of payment he was exposed to sale as a slave.

The third class of the inhabitants were the servants or slaves. This class was distinguished into two kinds :—1. Those who on account of poverty were obliged to go into service, and who were called Θῆτες and πελάται. These could change their masters at pleasure. —2. Those who were wholly in the power of their masters, and might be sold as any other kind of property. These were either such as had been taken prisoners in war, or bought of such as trafficked in them, or the descendants of those already in a state of bondage. The number of slaves (δοῦλοι) in Athens was very great. Even the poorer citizens had a slave for the care of their household affairs. They were treated generally with too much rigor, though at Athens their condition was much better than in any other Grecian city. If grievously oppressed, they could fly for refuge to the temple of Theseus, nor could any force them from it. If they were treated with too much severity and inhumanity, they could bring an action (ὕβρεως δίκη) against their masters, who were obliged to sell them to other citizens, if the fact were sufficiently proved. The slaves were not allowed to wear arms except in cases of extreme danger from an enemy, when they were sometimes armed for the defence of the state. Their punishments were very severe.

Section II.

Magistrates.

By the laws of Solon, no person could hold any office in the Athenian government unless he possessed considerable estates. This law was annulled by Aristides, who made every free citizen eligible to any office. Before a person could be nominated to any office, he was obliged to undergo an examination before the ἡλιασταί.* The magistrates were divided into three kinds, distinguished by the different methods of their election. 1. The χειροτονητοί, 'chirotoneti,' who received their office from the people, and who were so called because they were elected by the *holding up of hands*, (χειροτονία.) 2. The κληρωτοί, 'cleroti,' were chosen by lot, (κλῆροι,) drawn by the θεσμοθέται, who inscribed the name of every candidate on a tablet of brass, and put it into an urn with black and white beans, and those were elected whose tablets were drawn out with white

* See Section VI.

beans.   3. The ἁιρετοί, 'hæreti,' who were extraordinary officers, appointed by particular
tribes, to superintend any public affairs.   The
λογισταί, 'logistæ,' were those who examined
the public accounts, and were ten in number.

The first and most important of the magistracies was that of the ἄρχοντες, 'archons,' composed of nine of the principal citizens, whose
office was annual.   They were elected by the
votes of the citizens, but it was requisite that
they should be persons of good character, am-
ple fortune, and descendants from native citizens.   They were invested with the administration of the laws, and received all public in-
formations and complaints.   They were distinguished by name and office.   The first was
called the ἄρχων, 'archon,' by way of eminence,
and was president of the body.   His offices
were, to superintend some feasts, to take cognizance of lawsuits amongst relations, to protect orphans, and to regulate the dramatic entertainments.   The second was called the
βασιλεύς, 'king.'   It was his duty to assist in
the celebration of some festivals, to decide in
some religious causes, and to offer sacrifices
for the good of the state.   The third was called the πολεμαρχος, 'polemarch,' whose office
was, the management of war, and the jurisdiction over strangers.   The six other archons
were called the θεσμοθέται, 'thesmothetæ,' whose
duty it was to enforce the due observance of
the laws, and the execution of justice.

Each of the first three archons selected two assistants called πάρεδοι, to aid them in their duties. The εὔθυνοι, 'euthuni,' were ten officers appointed to assist the archons, to examine accounts, impose fines, &c.

The Eleven (οἱ ἕνδεκα) were elected from the ten tribes, one from each, which, together with their clerk, (γραμματεύς,) completed the number. Their duty was to arrest persons suspected of theft or robbery, and to put them to death if they confessed their guilt, otherwise to prosecute them in a judicial manner.

The φύλαρχοι, 'phylarchs,' were those who presided over the tribes, one over each. They took care of the public money of their tribes, and managed all their concerns.

The δήμαρχοι, 'demarchs,' were invested with a like power in the boroughs, (δῆμοι.)

The νομοθέται, 'nomothetæ,' were one thousand in number. Their office was not to enact new laws, but to inspect the old ones; and if they found any useless, or detrimental to the interests of the community, they caused them to be annulled by the people.

The πρεσβεῖς, 'ambassadors,' were chosen by the senate, and sometimes by the people, to treat with foreign states. Occasionally they were sent with full power to act as they should judge most conducive to the welfare and honor of the republic. But their power was generally restricted. They were usually attended by heralds, (κήρυκες,) who sometimes went on embassies themselves.

All the various magistrates, before entering upon their office, took a solemn oath to be faithful in discharging their duties. The archons were prohibited from receiving presents.

Section III.

Public Assemblies.

The Athenian Assembly (ἐκκλησία) was a meeting of all the citizens, (πολῖται,) with whom, when convoked according to law, were lodged all the interests of the state, such as taking cognizance of the enactments of the senate, making laws, appointing magistrates, declaring war, concluding peace, ratifying treaties and alliances, granting the freedom of the city to foreigners, &c. The assemblies were of two kinds; the ' ordinary,' (ἐκκλησία κυρία,) and the ' extraordinary,' (ἐκκλησία σύγκλητος.)

The ordinary assemblies were held four times every Prytanea,* on the 11th, 20th, 30th and 33d, of the thirty-six days that each class of the Prytanes (πρυτάνεις) were in office.

The extraordinary assemblies were summoned by the Prytanes, when any civil matters

* See Section IV.

were to be settled with greater dispatch than could be done in the ordinary assemblies. When any great calamity threatened the commonwealth, they were summoned by the στρατηγοι, the πολεμαρχοι, or the κηρυκες.

On account of the frequency of those assemblies, there was often a reluctance on the part of the citizens to attend them, and public officers (λογισταί) were appointed to compel their attendance. These officers closed all the gates excepting that which led to the meeting, and went through the forum, with cords dyed red, marking all whom they found there ; and those thus marked had a fine to pay.

The πρυτάνεις, the ἐπιστάτης, and the πρόεδροι had the management of these assemblies. The Prytanes always put up, in some conspicuous place, a public notice, (πρόγραμμα,) in which was an account of all the affairs to be discussed. The Proedri proposed to the people the subjects on which they were to deliberate. The Epistates was the president, and was chosen 'by lot from the Proedri. He gave the people permission to vote by a signal.

Before the assembly entered upon business, the place was purified by the sacrifice of a young pig. The public crier (κήρυξ) then ordered silence, and addressed a solemn prayer to the gods for knowledge and understanding necessary to wise deliberations. The subject to be considered (προβούλευμα) was then proposed by the Epistates, and those above fifty years of age were first invited to speak upon it, and afterwards any other citizens over thirty. The speaking being finished, the vote was taken, and this was generally done by the people's stretching forth their hands, (χειροτονία.) Sometimes they voted privately by pebbles, (ψῆφοι,) or beans, (κύαμοι,) which they cast into urns, (κάδοι.) The Proedri examined the votes, and proclaimed the result; and the decree (ψήφισμα) became a law. On the decree were written the name of the orator or senator who had given his opinion, and the name of the tribe to which the πρυτάνης belonged. Thus the supreme authority appears to have been lodged in the people.

The places of meeting for the assembly were the Forum, the Pnyx, or the Theatre of Bacchus. There were no fixed places for holding the extraordinary assemblies.

Section IV.

The Council or Senate of Five Hundred.

The people of Athens had, as we have seen, a very great share and authority in the government. In order that their decisions should be made with more wisdom and maturity, Solon instituted a council, or senate, consisting of four hundred members, afterwards increased by Clisthenes to five hundred, (ἡ βουλὴ ἡ τῶν πεντακοσίων.) This senate was composed of fifty persons· of the best character, elected from each of the ten tribes in the following manner. The Phylarch of every tribe handed in the name of every citizen of good character in his district over thirty years of age. These names were inscribed on small tablets (πινάκια) and put into an urn. Into another urn were put as many beans, fifty of which were white and the rest black. Those whose names were drawn out with the white beans were elected.

This senate assembled every day, except on the days appointed for the festivals. Each tribe in its turn furnished those who were to preside in it, called πρυτάνεις; and this rank was decided by lot. This presidency continued thirty-five or thirty-six days. This divided the Attic year into ten parts, each of which was called a πρυτανεία. These Prytanes, were divided into five committees of ten, each of which presided in turn one week, and the presidents of each week were called πρόεδροι. He who was president for the day was called επιστάτης, and presided in the senate, as well as in the assembly of the peole. He was intrusted with the public seal, as also with the keys of the citadel and treasury.

The senators, before they assembled, offered a sacrifice to Jupiter and Minerva. The president proposed the business that was to come before them. Every one was permitted to

give his opinion in his turn, always standing.
The act was then drawn up in writing and
read with a loud voice. Each senator then
gave his vote privately by putting a bean into
the urn. If the number of the white beans
exceeded the black, the question passed;
otherwise it was rejected. It was afterwards
laid before the assembly of the people, where,
if it was received and approved, it became a
law; if not, its force continued only one year.

The election of senators was annual. They
were the highest council of the nation, and
upon them devolved the whole care of the republic.

Section V.

The Court of Areopagus.

This court took its name from the place
where it held its meetings, which was upon
an eminence near the citadel, called Αρειοπάγος,
the Hill of Mars. This court was composed
of such members as had been archons. The
number of members was not fixed; at certain
times they amounted to two or three hundred.
They held their office during life, but before
they could be admitted, they had to undergo
a strict examination into their public and private characters; and if, after his admission,
any one was convicted of immorality, he was

expelled from the body. In consequence of this strictness in scrutinizing the character of its members, the judges of Areopagus sustained for centuries a merited reputation for wisdom, probity, and equity. It took cognizance of almost all crimes, vices, and immoralities; and all innovations, either in politics or in religion. To its care were committed the keeping and inspection of the laws, the management of the public funds, and the education of youth. Idleness, especially, it severely punished, and it had power to inquire into the occupation of every citizen of Athens.

The Areopagites ('Aρειοπαγίται) met almost daily, in the open air, and that they might not be influenced in their decisions by the sight of the parties engaged in the suit, they held their meetings at night. The trials were preceded by imposing and solemn ceremonies. Sacrifices were offered, and the two parties, placed amid the victims, took a most solemn oath, calling down the vengeance of heaven upon themselves and their families if they testified falsely. The accused then seated himself upon the stone called ἀναίδεια, 'impudence;' or ἀναιτία, 'innocence;' and the accuser upon the one called ὕβρις, 'injury.' The advocates for either party were not allowed to make any appeal to the passions of the judges, but were required to state the simple facts, and accompany their statements with proof. The judges gave their opinions secretly. They voted with black and white flints; and that these might be distinguished in the dark, holes were made in the black, but not in the white. The white acquitted; the black condemned. These they put into two urns; the white into 'the urn of mercy,' (ὁ ἐλέου,) the black into 'the urn of death,' (ὁ θανάτου.) If the votes were equal, an inferior officer put one into the urn of mercy in favor of the accused.

Section VI.

Other Courts of Justice, and Judicial Proceedings.

There were different tribunals, according to the different nature of the matters to be adjudged; but appeals might be brought to the people from all decrees of the other judges. There were ten courts of justice besides the Areopagus, four of which took cognizance of actions in which blood was concerned, (ἐπὶ τῶν φονικῶν πραγμάτων,) and the other six, of civil matters, (ἐπὶ τῶν δημοτικῶν.) One court (ἐπὶ Παλλαδίῳ) took cognizance of cases of unintentional homicides; another, (the ἐπὶ Δελφινίῳ,) of such murders as were confessed to be committed by permission of the laws, as in cases of self-defence; and another, (ἐπὶ Πρυτανείῳ,) of cases of death where the party had been killed by inanimate things, such as trees, stones, &c.

The most celebrated court in civil affairs

was the ἡλιαία, which was held in the open air,
and exposed to the sun's rays, whence its name,
(from ἥλιος, 'the sun.')   The judges of the court
were called ἡλιασταί, ' heliastæ ;' their number
was not always the same, being greater or
smaller according to the importance of the
cause.   When a person wished to bring an
action against any one, he took his name to a
magistrate, and if the cause was of a proper
kind to be brought into a court of justice, the
plaintiff (διώκων) summoned the defendant (φεύ-
γων) to appear before the magistrate by a bai-
liff, (κλητής.)   Then the parties met before the
magistrate with their witnesses, and the plaintiff took an oath (προωμοσία) to bring no false
accusation, and the defendant took an oath
(ἀντωμοσία) that his answer should be true, or
that he was innocent.

Before the trial commenced each party was
obliged to deposit a certain sum of money (πρυ-
τανεῖα) with the magistrate who presented the
cause in court.   A fine (ἐπωβελία) was imposed
on those who could not prove the indictment
they had presented.   The public crier (κῆρυξ)
opened the court by reading the indictment.
If the accused did not appear, judgment was
passed upon him, and if he did not within ten
days come and show sufficient excuse for absence, this sentence was valid.   The indictment before conviction was called αἰτία ; after
conviction, ἔλεγχος ; and after the sentence, ἀδί-
κημα.

Witnesses were required to swear to the fact, to deny it, or that they knew any thing about it, or to pay a fine of 1000 drachms, ($167.) None but citizens were admitted as witnesses. Slaves were allowed to give evidence only when examined by torture.

The parties pleaded their cause either in person, or employed advocates to do it for them. The time allowed for the hearing was generally fixed, and a water-clock (κλεψύδρα) regulated its duration. The judges then brought in their verdict. This was given by sea-shells, (χοιρίναι,) or pebbles, (ψῆφοι,) or beans, (κύαμοι.) If there was a greater number of the white beans, the accused was acquitted: if a majority of the black, he was condemned. If he was found guilty of a capital crime, he was delivered into the hands of ' the Eleven' (ὁι ἕνδεκα) for punishment. If sentenced to pay a fine, he was delivered to the ' collectors,' (πράκτορες;) and if unable to pay it, he was con demned to perpetual imprisonment.

Section VII.

Judgments and Accusations.

The judgments among the Athenians were of two kinds;—1. Public, (δημοτικαί,) such as referred to crimes which injured more immediately the republic, called κατηγορίαι ;—2. Private, (ἰδιωτικαί,) which comprised all disputes between individuals, and were called δίκαι.

The accusation called γραφὴ was that preferred against those who were charged with any of the following crimes :—φόνος, 'murder,' which was punished with death ;—τραῦμα ἐκ προνοίας, 'a wound inflicted intentionally ;'— πυρκαϊά, 'arson ;'—φάρμακον, 'poison ;'—βούλευσις, 'conspiracy ;'—ἱεροσυλία, 'sacrilege ;'—ἀσέβεια, 'impiety ;'—προδοσία, 'treason ;'—ἀστρατεία, 're-fusing to serve in war ;'—λειποστράτιον, 'deser-tion from the army ;'—λειποτάξιον, 'leaving one's post ;'—δειλία, 'cowardice ;'—λειποναύτιον, 'deser-tion from the fleet ;'—τὸ ῥίψαι τὴν ἀσπίδα, 'losing one's shield.'

The judgment called φάσις was the detection and information given of any secret and concealed crime. Ἐισαγγελία was the name of the process instituted against those who committed crimes against which there was no express law. It generally referred to great public offences, by which the state was endangered.

Amongst the private judgments were ἀδίκου δίκη, 'action for injury ;'—κατηγορίας δίκη, 'action for slander ;'—αἰκίας δίκη, 'action for assault ;'— κλοπῆς δίκη, 'action for theft ;' which last was punished with death, if committed upon any of the public temples, altars, or gymnasia. But if one was convicted of stealing from a private person, he was obliged to make restitution to double the amount of the property stolen, and was moreover punished with infamy, (ἀτιμια.)

Section VIII.

Punishments and Rewards.

Of the punishments not capital among the Athenians, the principal were these ;—1. Ζημία, which means any punishment, but often signified any pecuniary ' fine ;'—2. 'Ατιμία, ' infamy,' or public disgrace, and loss of all honors, and public offices ;—3. Δουλεία, ' servitude,' which could be inflicted only on the ἄτιμοι, 'the disgraced,' the foreigners, and freed servants ; —4. Στίγματα, 'brand-marks,' which were made with a red-hot iron on the foreheads or hands of runaway slaves, or any notorious malefactor ;—5. Στήλη, 'the pillar,' on which was recorded the crime of the offender, and then exposed to public view ;—6. Δεσμοί, ' chains' or ' fetters,' and δεσμωτήριον, ' prison ;'—7. Φυγή, ' exile,' but the exiled person could be recalled by the same power that banished him ;—8. 'Οστρακισμός, ' ostracism.' This last differed from ' exile' (φυγή) in these respects ; the exiled were banished from their country forever, and their property confiscated ; but the sentence of the ostracised was limited to ten years, after which they could return and enjoy their estates, which were, in the mean time, preserved for them. The process of this ostracising was as follows. Every man took 'a shell,' (ὄστρακον,) and having marked upon it the name of the person whom he wished to banish, carried it to a certain part of the forum. When the people had finished giving in their votes, the archons counted all the shells, and if less than six thousand, the ostracism was void. But if not, they sorted them according to the names written upon them, and he whose name had been written by the majority, had the sentence of banishment pronounced upon him.

Death (Θάνατος) was inflicted upon criminals in various ways:—1. Ξίφος, 'the sword,' by beheading ;—2. Βρόχος, 'the rope,' by hanging or strangling ;—3. Φάρμακον, ' poison' ;—4. Κρημνός, ' a precipice,' from which the criminal was thrown;—5. Τύμπανα, ' clubs' of wood, with which he was beaten to death ;—6. Σταυρός, ' the cross,' upon which the criminal was nailed ;—7. Βάραθρον, 'a deep pit,' with sharp spikes at the top to prevent the escape of the condemned, and others at the bottom to pierce and torture him ;—8. Λιθοβολια, ' lapidation,' or stoning to death ;—9. Καταποντισμός, ' drowning ;' —10. Πυρ, ' burning.'

While the laws inflicted the severest penalties upon offenders, in order to deter men from the commission of crime, they, on the other hand, conferred honors and rewards on those

S

who merited them by the practice of great and illustrious deeds. The following were the principal rewards :—1. Προεδρία, 'the first place' at all exhibitions, banquets, and public meetings.—2. Εἰκών, 'a picture' or 'statue' erected in some public place in the city.—3. Στέφανοι, 'crowns' of various materials. —4. Ἀτέλεια, 'immunity from taxes,' except from such as were required for carrying on war, and building ships, from which no man was excused except the nine archons.—5. Σιτία, παρασιτία σίπησις εν Πρυτανείω, 'a public dinner or entertainment in the Prytaneum,' given to those who had done distinguished service to the republic, and particularly to those who had been ambassadors, (πρεσβεῖς.) When Athens enjoyed her highest glory it was uncommon to bestow these honors ; but afterwards they became more common, and consequently less valued.

Section IX.

Revenues and Administration of Finance.

The revenues of the Athenians are generally classed under four heads.—1. The duties (τέλη) arising from agriculture, the sale of woods, the produce of the silver mines, the duties upon the export and import of merchandise, and the taxes upon property and foreigners.—2. The tributes of the allied or subjected states, (φόροι.)—3. The extraordinary taxes levied in pressing occasions and emergencies, as war, &c., (ἐισφορά.)—4. The fines (τιμήματα) imposed upon persons by the judges for various misdemeanors, and the proceeds of confiscated property, (δημιόπρατα.) A tenth part of these was consecrated to Minerva, and a fiftieth to the other divinities. The tributes of the allies (φόροι) was by far the most productive source of revenue. The mines were farmed to individuals, and worked by slaves. The commerce of the Athenians was considerable.

These different revenues were expended in paying the troops; building and fitting out fleets; erecting, repairing, and adorning public edifices, temples, walls, forts, and citadels; celebrating festivals and games, maintaining the poor and infirm, (ἀδύνατοι,) and the orphans whose fathers fell in battle; and paying salaries of officers.

All the regular expenditures and revenues were settled by laws enacted by the people. The senate superintended the different branches of public economy. The officers subordinate to the senate were—1. The πωλῆται, 'poletæ,' those to whose care was intrusted every thing that the state sold or farmed out. They were ten in number. Under these Poletæ were assessors (ἐπιγραφεῖς) and collectors, (ἐκλογείς.)—2. The ἀποδέκται, 'treasurers' or 're-

228 ANTIQUITIES OF GREECE.

ceivers,' as also 'disbursers.' These were also ten in number.—3. The γραμματεύς and ἀντιγραφεῖς, 'the secretary' and 'clerks' of the treasury.

Distinct from any of these officers was the 'Treasurer of the Public Revenue," (ταμίας, or ἐπιμελιτὴς ϛῆς κοινῆς προσόδου,) the most important of all the officers of finance, who was chosen by the vote of the people. His office was quadrennial. All the money that was received or expended passed through his hands or under his inspection.

All persons to whom duties were let, and who had leases of the public revenues, were called ϛελῶναι, 'publicans' or 'farmers.' They were obliged to be persons in good credit, and to give bonds endorsed by other persons as security for the payment of the money due on their leases. If they failed to pay at a stipulated time, they forfeited double the amount of the bond ; and if they failed entirely, they with their sureties were committed to prison, and their property confiscated.

Section X.

The Council of the Amphictyons.

The celebrated Council of the Amphictyons is introduced here, though it was not peculiar to the Athenians, but common to all Greece.

This council was a general congress of the

states and cities of Greece.   The institution is attributed to Amphictyon, king of Athens, who gave it his name.   It was composed of deputies, originally sent from twelve states or districts into which Greece was divided.   Each state sent two deputies.   The number of deputies was consequently twenty-four ; but it was afterwards increased to thirty.   They met twice a year, in the spring and autumn, sometimes at Thermopylæ, and sometimes at Delphi ; and, if affairs required, they met more frequently.

The object of the institution of this council was to unite in a sacred fellowship the several nations of Greece which were represented in it, and to take measures for mutual protection from danger.   The Amphictyons were also the protectors of the oracle of Delphi, and the guardians of the vast riches of that temple. They had full power to discuss and determine in all differences which might arise between the Amphictyonic cities, and to fine the culpable nation in heavy penalties.   They could employ not only the rigor of the laws in the execution of their decrees, but even raise troops, if it was necessary, to compel such as rebelled to submit to them.

The influence of this council was very salutary.   The deputies from all parts of Greece, thus meeting together to consult for their common interest, could not but see the importance of union and harmony for the prosperity and preservation of their several states.

CHAPTER III.

CIVIL GOVERNMENT OF THE LACEDÆMONIANS.

Section I.

Inhabitants of Laconia.

The Leleges were generally regarded as the original inhabitants of Laconia. Afterwards the descendants of Hercules, together with the Dorians, overran the country, and imposed tributes upon the original cities, all of which submitted excepting Helos; but this was soon conquered, and its inhabitants reduced to slavery. Here was the origin of that large body of slaves among the Lacedæmonians, called Helots, (Εἴλωτες.)

Sparta was but little known among the states of Greece until the time of Lycurgus, its great legislator. He divided the people into five tribes—1. The Limnatæ, (Λιηνάται;) 2. The Cynosureans, (Κυνοσουρεῖς;)—3. The Pitanatæ, (Πιτανάται;)—4. The Ægidæ, ('Αιγεῖδαι;) and 5. The Messoatæ, (Μεσσοάται.)

The citizens were of two kinds: those who were born such, and those who were presented

with the freedom of the city. In the early peri
ods of the Spartan history, in order that the num
ber of inhabitants might be increased, all stran
gers were admitted to the privilege of citizenship, but subsequently the freedom of the city
was more sparingly bestowed. Children were
considered as the property of the state, and
parents were not permitted to educate them
as they pleased. As soon as a child was born,
it was taken to a place called Lesche, (Λέσχη,)
where the most aged persons of the tribe assembled to examine it. If it appeared well
formed and healthy, orders were given for its
education, and some portion of public land was
assigned to it. But if it did not seem of a
healthy and vigorous constitution, it was
thrown into a gulf called 'Αποθέται.

At the age of seven the boys were enrolled
in the classes called ἀγέλαι; at the age of
eighteen they left the company of boys, and
were admitted into that of the ἔφηβοι, or young
men. At the age of thirty they were classed
among the men, (ἔξηβοι,) and were allowed to
undertake public offices.

The inhabitants of the city were called
Σπαρτιαταὶ, and enjoyed peculiar rights and
privileges. The inhabitants of the country
(Περίοικοι) were in some respects subject to the
citizens, yet were governed by the same laws,
and were equally eligible to the different offices of state. The freemen of Sparta were
divided into two classes, the ὅμοιοι, 'equals,' and

the ὑπομείνες, 'inferiors.' The former could vote and enjoy all the honors of the state; the latter could vote, but were not eligible to office.

The slaves were of two kinds, the δοῦλοι, who had been reduced to servitude, and the οἰκέται, who were born in slavery. The Helots (Ἔιλωτες) were distinguished from the slaves properly so called, since they had rather a middle rank between slaves and citizens. They greatly exceeded in number the freemen, and were to them a continual object of fear. The severest cruelties were inflicted upon them in order to keep them in subjection. They wore a particular kind of dress, that they might be more readily distinguished. They were employed in cultivating the lands, and in the various mechanic arts. They served as sailors on board the fleet; and in the army every heavy-armed soldier (ὁπλίτης) was attended by one or more of them.

The whole population of Laconia was about 270,000; of whom the Helots formed about four-fifths of the entire number.

Section II.

Magistrates of Sparta. The Kings. The Senate. The Ephori.

The government of Sparta was vested in the Kings, the Senate, and the Ephori. There were two kings, (ἀρχαγέται,) and hence the established government was called a diarchy, (διαρχή.) Euristhenes and Procles, twin sons of one of the kings of Laconia, succeeded to the throne of their father with equal authority, and they thus became the progenitors of a double line of kings. The power of the kings was extremely limited, especially in the city, and in time of peace. In war they had the command of the fleet and army. They were the chief directors in all matters pertaining to religion. They presided in the senate, and had each a vote there which was considered as equal to two. They appeared in public without a retinue or any display.

The senate·(γερουσία) consisted of the two kings and twenty-eight wise and aged men, (γέροντες,) and was the supreme council of Sparta. No person could become a senator who had not been distinguished for his bravery and virtues, and arrived at the age of sixty years. The senators continued in office during life. All public business was proposed and examined in the senate, and by it decrees were passed. But such decrees were not valid unless ratified by the people.

The whole executive power of Sparta was vested in the Ephori, (ἔφοροι.) They were five in number. They could check and restrain the authority of the kings, and even imprison them, if guilty of irregularities. They had the management of the public money, and were the arbiters of peace and war. Their office was annual. They alone could summon the assemblies of the people, collect their suffrages, and dissolve them. Citizens of every age and rank were subject to their inspection, and were amenable to their jurisdiction.

Among the inferior magistrates were the βειδιαῖοι, who presided over the games called Platanista; the νομοφύλακες, 'guardians of the laws,' who rewarded or punished persons according to law; the παιδόνομοι, persons who superintended the boys placed under their care at seven years of age; the πολέμαρχοι, those who under the kings commanded the army; the ἁρμόσυνοι, who observed the lives and manners of the Spartan women, and saw that the games and exercises were conducted with decorum : the προξένοι, who extended their care to strangers and foreign ambassadors.

Section III.

Public Assemblies.

There were two public assemblies which convened at Sparta. The greater assembly (ἐκκλησία) was composed of the kings, the senators, and deputies chosen by all the inhabitants of Laconia. In this assembly were discussed all matters of great public interest.

The less assembly (μικρὰ ἐκκλησία) consisted only of the citizens of Sparta, and was held every month. It had the power of electing all the magistrates, and of ratifying decrees of the senate. Every Spartan capable of bearing arms could be present at this assembly; but he must have passed the age of thirty, before he was permitted to give his opinion on any subject. The Ephori convened and presided at every meeting. The place where the assembly met was in the open air, near the river Cnacion. The king and senators frequently gave their opinion, and also the Ephori. The question was decided by acclamation, *viva voce.* If, however, after repeated trials the majority could not be ascertained, the two parties divided, and were counted.

Section IV.

Rewards and Punishments.

Honor was highly prized by the Spartan. He was taught from infancy to aspire after the reputation of a man of heroic valor, and unimpeachable virtue. The Ephori were accustomed to appoint three officers, (ἱππαγρέται,) each of whom selected one hundred men as chosen guards (λογάδες) from the best citizens; and to be elected in this number, was considered as the first honor in the city. The assemblies paid the honor of rising up in the presence of the aged. The προέδρα, 'first seat' in an assembly, was esteemed very honorable. Olive crowns were given as a reward for brave deeds. Statues and monuments, though not of a very costly kind, were erected in honor of the most distinguished.

Among the punishments were, 1. Ζημια, 'a pecuniary fine,' which, if not paid, the person fined was driven into banishment;—2. Κλοιὸς, 'a collar of wood,' which went round the neck and fastened the hands;—3. Μαστίγωσις, 'whipping;'—4. Κέντησις, 'goading;'—5. 'Ασιμία, 'infamy' or 'disgrace;'—6. Φυγὴ, 'banishment,' generally for the avoiding of penalties;—7. Βρόχος, 'strangling,' with a rope;—8. Θάνατος, 'death,' which was esteemed by the Spartans the mildest form of punishment. The infamy (ἀτιμία) was deemed more formidable than death. The 'disgraced' (ἄτιμοι) were general-ly those who had fled in battle. They were deprived of citizenship, compelled to go naked through the forum in winter, and to suffer themselves to be beaten by any one whom they might meet. Death (θάνατος) was not in-flicted in public, but in the night, and in a certain part of the prison called δεκάς

CHAPTER IV.

MILITARY AND NAVAL AFFAIRS OF THE GREEKS.

Section I.

Manner of Declaring War, and Levying Soldiers

BEFORE the Greeks engaged in war, they published a declaration of their injuries, and demanded satisfaction through their ambas-sadors, (πρεσβεις.) If the demands were not complied with, they sent heralds, (κήρυκες,) who gave orders to the enemy to prepare for an invasion, and who sometimes threw a spear towards them in token of defiance. But the Greeks never engaged in war without encouragement from the gods. The soothsayers and oracles were consulted, and no expense was spared to enlist the gods in their favor. They offered sacrifices and made great vows, which were to be fulfilled upon the event of the success of their undertaking. Some particular seasons were esteemed more favorable for a military enterprise than others. An eclipse, or the appearance of a comet, would often deter them from marching, or engaging in battle. The Athenians would not march before 'the seventh day,' (ἐντὸς ἑδδόμης,) because this day was considered more favorable than others. But the Lacedæmonians were the most scrupulous on this point. They never would march until the full moon ; for they thought that this planet had a special influence over their affairs, and when at the full, that it prospered their undertakings.

The Grecian armies consisted of citizens, allies, mercenaries, and sometimes of slaves. The laws obliged every citizen, except the farmers of the public revenue, (τελῶναι,) to appear in arms when summoned by a proper magistrate. No rank or station exempted any others from military service between the ages of eighteen and sixty. It was only, however, on extraordinary occasions, that the Athenians were required to serve in the army after the age of forty-five. The Athenians were not

generally sent beyond the limits of Attica until twenty years of age; and the Spartans
were not usually sent to foreign wars until
thirty.   Citizens were obliged to enrol their
names in a public register as soon as they arrived at the age of eighteen years, and the
general could summon any of those thus enrolled, to accompany him, after the people had
determined to engage in a military expedition.
This levy was called καταγραφὴ, κατάλογος, or
ϛατολογία.   As soon as the youthful soldier was
enrolled, he took the military oath, (ὁρκομοσία,)
and then enjoyed all the privileges, and was
subject to the duties of a citizen.   In early
times the soldiers were at their own expense,
but after the time of Pericles they were paid.

SECTION II.

Different sorts of Soldiers;—their Armor, and Arms.

   The Grecian armies were composed of three
kinds of soldiers;—1. τὸ πεζικόν, 'the infantry,'
or 'foot soldiers;'—2. τὸ ἐπ' οχημάτων, 'those
who fought from chariots;'—3. τὸ ἐφ' ἵππων, 'the
cavalry' or 'horsemen.'   The main strength
was in the infantry, for it greatly exceeded in
number the other classes.
   The infantry was divided into three classes,
the ὁπλῖται, the ψιλοί, and the πελταϛαί.   The

ὁπλῖται, 'heavy-armed soldiers,' were designed for close fight. They wore heavy armor, and engaged with broad shields and long spears. They were placed in the centre of the army, and were arranged, generally, sixteen deep, and were furnished with a pike twenty-one feet long. In marching, every soldier occupied a space of six feet, but in advancing upon an enemy the ranks (ταξεῖς) closed, and were not more than a foot or two distant from each other.

The ψιλοί, 'light-armed soldiers,' fought with arrows, darts, javelins, and slings, and were stationed either in the van to begin the combat, or on the wings, to annoy the enemy's cavalry. They were below the ὁπλῖται in point of dignity.

The πελτασται, 'targeteers,' were so called from a small shield (πέλτη) which they bore. They held a middle rank between the ὁπλῖται and the ψιλοί, and were generally placed on the wings.

The practice of fighting from chariots was very ancient among the Greeks. Their chariots of war were drawn by two horses, but sometimes a third was added as leader, and was called σειραφόρος, because he governed the reins. Every chariot contained two men, one who was charioteer or driver, (ἡνίοχος,) and the other the warrior, (παραιβάτης,) who directed where to drive. There were chariots 'armed with scythes,' (δρεπανηφόροι,) with which whole ranks of soldiers were cut down.

The cavalry was esteemed the most honorable service, particularly in the Athenian army.
The number of the cavalry among the Athenians
was small, being generally about one tenth of
the number of the heavy-armed soldiers. The
Spartan cavalry was still smaller in number.
The Thessalonians had the largest number of
cavalry. The horsemen had a variety of names,
mostly derived from their armor or different
modes of fighting.

After the time of Alexander the Great, elephants were sometimes employed by the
Greeks in battle. They bore large towers,
which contained from ten to thirty soldiers,
who harassed the enemy with missile weapons. But, though they often spread terror
through the ranks of the enemy, they could
not always be depended upon with certainty;
for they were very unmanageable, and sometimes even would turn upon their own party.

The armor, or *defensive weapons* of the
Greeks, was generally made of brass, and covered with frightful images. The helmet
(περικεφαλαία, κόρυς, κράνος) was generally made of
the skins of beasts, and received various
names, according to the names of the different
animals, as λεοντέη, 'of lion's skin;' ταυρεία, ' of
bull's hide,' &c. These skins were always
worn with the hair on them, and often the teeth
of the animal were exposed, in order to inspire
the more terror. The crest of the helmet
(λόφος) was generally of horse-hair, and from

T

this circumstance the helmet itself is often called ἵππουρις, ἱπποχαίτης, &c.

The cuirass or breastplate (θώραξ) consisted of two parts, one of which was a defence to the breast, the other to the back. It was sometimes made of leather, and of small twisted cords, but generally of brass, or some other metal.

The girdle or belt (ζώνα or ζῶμα) met the breastplate, and was a great defence to the lower part of the body. The greaves (κνημῖδες) were made of metal, and were used to defend the legs, the sides being closed with clasps.

The shield or buckler (ασπίς) was sometimes made of wood, but generally of hides doubled into several folds, and strengthened by plates of metal. The boss (ὀμφαλός) was a prominent part in the middle. The Grecian shields were generally sufficiently large to defend the whole body. Their shape was usually round. The πέλτη was a small and light shield in the form of a half moon.

The arms, or *offensive weapons*, of the Greeks were,—1. Ἔγχος and δόρυ, 'the spear,' or 'pike,' made of wood and pointed with metal;—2. Ξίφος, 'the sword,' which was hung in a belt which extended round the shoulders, and reached down to the thighs. Near it hung the dagger, παραμήριον, μάχαιρα ;—3. Ἀξίνη, πέλεκυς, 'the battle-axe,' or 'pole-axe ;'—4. Τόξον, 'the bow,' and Βέλη, ὀιστοί, ἰοί, 'arrows ;'—5. Ακόντια, 'darts or javelins ;'—6. Σφενδόνη, 'the sling ;'—7. Πυροβόλοι λίθοι, 'fire-balls,' which were made of wood, with spikes of iron, and to which were placed torches, hemp, pitch, and other combustible matter. These were ignited and hurled with great force into the ranks of the enemy.

The μάγγανα or μηχαναι were arms or ma· chines; used in sieges. There were several kinds of these. The κλίμακες, 'scaling-ladders,' were the oldest of these machines. The κριός, 'battering-ram,' was an engine with an iron head, resembling a ram's head, which was employed in battering down the walls of the enemy. The common length of the battering-ram was about a hundred feet. It was generally suspended by the middle, with ropes or chains fastened to a beam which lay across two posts; and hanging thus equally balanced, it was violently thrust forward, drawn back, and again pushed forward, until by repeated strokes it had broken down the wall. The ἐλέπολις, 'city-taker,' resembled the battering ram, but was much larger. It was covered, and driven with ropes and wheels. The χελώνη, *testudo*, or 'tortoise,' was so called from its covering the soldiers as a tortoise is covered by its shell. It was usually formed by the soldiers placing their shields, one over the other, in such a manner as to protect them completely from the missiles, when they approached the walls of the enemy. Καταπέλται denote sometimes arrows, and sometimes the engines from which they were cast. Λιθοβόλοι and πετροβόλοι were engines for hurling stones.

Section III.

Military Officers, Division and Forms of the Army.

In those states which were governed by kings, it was customary for the king himself to lead the army; but on some occasions he might nominate a person of distinguished worth and valor to be his general, (πολέμαρχος.)

At Athens each of the ten tribes nominated a commander (στρατηγός) from their own body. Each of these ten generals was invested with equal power, and during any military enterprise, they commanded alternately, each of them for a day. This practice of sending so many generals of equal power was discontinued after the time of Pericles. One or two of the ten generals were appointed to conduct the affairs of the army, while the remainder superintended various religious ceremonies at home.

The ten tribes also each elected a ταξίαρχος, who was in rank inferior only to the general, (στατηγόος.) They had the care of arranging the army before battle, of fixing the place for encampment, and of deciding upon the route for the march. The ἔππαρχοι, 'generals of the horsemen,' were two in number, and had under them ten φύλαρχοι, who were nominated by the ten tribes. There were other inferior officers, who took their names from the band or number of men under their command, as the λοχανοί, χιλίαρχοι, &c.

At Sparta, there was but one general, who was usually one of the kings. He was accompanied by some of the Ephori, who assisted him with their counsel.

Among the Greeks, the whole army, including both horse and foot, was called στατία; the front or van, μέτωπον, or πρῶτος ζυγός; the wings, κέρατα; and the rear, ἔσχατος ζυγός, or ὄυρα. The πεμπάς was a band of five soldiers, and its leader was called πεμπάδαρχος. The λόχος consisted of sixteen soldiers, though sometimes it included more than that number. The συλλοχισμός was a union of several λόχοι. The ἑκατονταρχία consisted of eight λόχοι, or one hundred and twenty-eight men. Its leader was called ἑκατόνταρχος. In every ἑκατονταρχία there were five attendants called ἔκτακτοι, from their not serving in the ranks. They were—1. The στρατοκήρυξ, 'the crier' or 'herald,' who conveyed the word of command;—2. The σημειοφόρος, 'the ensign,' who gave the officers commands by signs when the noise of battle drowned the voice of the herald;—3. The σαλπιγκτής, 'the trumpeter,' who signified to the soldiers the will of their officers when the noise rendered the two former attendants useless;—4. The ὑπηρέτης, 'the servant,' who waited upon the soldiers to supply them with necessaries;—5. The οὐραγός, 'the lieutenant,' who brought up the rear, and took care that none of the soldiers deserted, or were left behind.

The term φάλαγξ was generally applied to the whole army drawn up in order of battle. Μῆκος φάλαγγος was the whole length of the army from wing to wing; βάθος φάλαγγος was its depth or extent from van to rear; ζυγοὶ φαλαγγος were the ranks taken according to the length of the phalanx; στίχοι, or λόχοι, were the files measured according to its depth; πλαγία φαλαγξ was when it was broad in front and narrow in flank; αμφίστομος φαλαγξ was when the soldiers were placed back to back, that they might face the enemy on every side when they were in danger of being surrounded.

The ἔμβολον, 'the wedge,' was the army drawn up in the form of the letter Δ, and the κοιλεμβολον, 'shears,' was the wedge reversed and without a base, in the form of a letter V, designed to receive the attack of the wedge. The term πλαίσιον was generally used when the army was drawn up in the form of a square. The ἴλη represented the figure of an egg, in which form the Thessalians usually arranged their cavalry. It is generally used for a troop of horse of any form and number.

The Lacedæmonian army was divided into regiments (μόραι) which consisted of about four

hundred men. Over every μόρα was a commander, called πολέμαρχος.

Section IV.

*Battles, Signals, Treatment of the Slain, &c.
Military Punishments and Rewards.*

The Greeks never engaged in battle without having implored the favor of the gods by
prayer and sacrifices.   They also always re-
freshed themselves with food before engaging.
The commanders then marshalled the army
in order of battle, and the general addressed
the soldiers, exhorting them to exert their utmost courage and strength against their enemies.   They then sang the hymn to Mars,
(παιάν,) and rushed to the engagement, with a
general war-shout (ἀλαλαγμός) of the word
ἀλαλά.

The σύμβολα, 'signals,' were of two kinds,
those pronounced by the mouth, and those visible to the eye.   The σύνθημα, 'the watchword,'
was communicated by the general to the subordinate officers.

Another kind of signal, the σημεῖα, were ensigns or flags, the elevation of which was a
sign to join battle, and the lowering of it, to
desist.

The Greeks did not treat the dead bodies of
their enemies with the least respect. They
permitted them to remain on the field without
interment, and would not even permit the
conquered to bury their own dead without
paying large sums for their ransom. But
they were scrupulously careful to pay every
honor to the bodies of their own soldiers who
had lost their lives in fighting for their country; and it was deemed highly criminal to
neglect to perform any funeral rites over them.
Tombs were erected over them, on which were
generally inscribed their names and exploits.
If they had fallen in battle in a distant country, their bodies were burned, and the ashes
collected, and brought home to their relations,
and deposited in the tombs of their ancestors.

The prisoners who could not ransom themselves were made slaves. The spoils (ἔναρα) were
garments, arms, &c.; which if taken from the
dead were called σκῦλα, if from the living, λάφυρα.
The general selected from the spoils what he
preferred, and distributed the rest among others who had signalized themselves in the battle. The Lacedæmonians, however, were forbidden to take the spoils of those whom they
had vanquished, esteeming it unworthy to be
enriched by them. The best of the spoils were
made an offering to the gods, either by con-
suming them with fire, or suspending them in
their temples.

The commander generally punished the soldiers for any delinquency as he thought proper. But in some cases the laws made provision. Deserters (αὐτομόλοι) were punished with death. Those who refused to serve in war, (ἀστράτευτοι,) those who quitted their ranks, (λειποτάκται,) and cowards, (δειλοί,) were obliged to sit three days in the forum, clothed in female apparel; and had also a fine imposed upon them. Those who lost their shield were fined.

As rewards of valor, private soldiers were invested with office, and the subordinate officers were promoted. To some, crowns were presented, and others had the liberty of erecting statues to the gods, with inscriptions indicating their victory. Those who became disabled in the service of their country (ἀδύνατοι) were maintained at the public expense, if poor; and the children of those who had fallen in battle were educated at the charge of the state.

Section V.

Different Kinds of Ships; with their Parts. Ornaments, &c.

The ships were of two kinds,—ships of war, (νῆες,) and ships of commerce or merchant-men, (ὁλκάδες πλοῖα.) The former were long and narrow, and generally rowed with oars; the lat-

U

ter were of an oval form, and in order to carry a greater quantity of commodities, were very wide in the middle, and had very broad bottoms. They were usually propelled with sails. The ships of war at first had but one rank of rowers on a side, but afterwards they had two, three, four, and more benches of rowers on each side. These benches were placed above one another not in a vertical line, so as not to interfere with the rowers in the other benches. The Athenians generally used the triremes, (τριήρεις,) which contained three benches of rowers. These benches were called τοῖχοι and ἐδώλια.

The principal parts of a ship were the prow (πρώρα;) the hull or hold, (μεσόκοιλος;) and the stern, (πρύμνα.) The prow (or *fore-deck*) was generally adorned with paintings, and different sculptures of gods, men, or animals. There were ornaments also on the stern.

The rudder (πηδάλιον) was fixed on the side of the hindermost deck, near the stern, but not directly in it. It resembled an oar in shape, but was longer, and broader at the extremity. In very large vessels, two rudders were sometimes used, one of which was placed near the prow.

The anchor (ἄγκυρα) was originally a large stone bored through the middle; but afterwards those of iron were used, made very much like our modern anchors. Every ship had several masts, (ἱστοι.)

The beak (ἔμβολον) was of wood, strengthened with brass, and fixed to the prow in order to injure the ships of the enemy. There were also coverings (καταφράγματα) erected for the purpose of protecting the soldiers from the missiles of the enemy.

Section VI.

Naval Officers, Mariners, and Naval Engagements.

The naval officers were of two kinds; those who had charge of the whole crew and commanded the vessel; and those who commanded the soldiers. The ἀρχικυβερνήτης, 'captain,' was the principal officer, and had the direction of all marine affairs, and of the course of the whole fleet. The κυβερνήτης, 'pilot,' had the care of the ship and the sailors. He sat in the stern to steer.

The officer who commanded the soldiers or marines, was called τριήραρχος, 'captain of a trireme galley;' and the commander of the whole fleet, στόλαρχος, ναύαρχος, or στρατηγός, 'the admiral,' whose power was unlimited, and whose continuance in command depended on the will of the people. The ἐπιστολεύς was the vice-admiral, and commanded under the admiral.

The ships of war were furnished with row
ers, (ἐρέται, κωπηλώται;) sailors or mariners,
(ναῦται;) and soldiers or marines, (ἐπιβάται.)
The condition of the rowers was very hard
and laborious.   The sailors were exempted
from rowing, but had the care of the sails,
ropes, &c.   The soldiers were in general armed in the same manner as the land forces.

In preparing for a naval action, the Greeks
cleared the ships of every thing not necessary
for the fight.   As soon as the enemy appeared they lowered the sails, took down the masts,
and managed the vessel entirely by oars.

The admiral's ship gave the signal for engaging by hanging out a gilded shield.   During the elevation of this signal the battle continued; and the ships were directed what to
do by particular movements of the shield.   A
grappling iron (χεὶρ σιδηρὰ) was used for fasten-
ing the ships to each other.

CHAPTER V.

Section I.

The Grecian Deities,—Sacred Places and Persons.

The Grecian religion was idolatry in its grossest and widest acceptation. Their deities (θεοί) were divided into the celestial, (ἐπουράνιοι,) the terrestrial, (ἐπιχθόνιοι,) and the infernal, (καταχθόνιοι.) In this last class were also included the marine deities, (θαλάσσιοι.) The twelve 'great gods,' μεγάλοι θεοί, were Jupiter, (Ζεύς,) Neptune, (Ποσειδῶν,) Mars, ("Αρης,) Apollo, ('Απόλλων,) Vulcan, ("Ηφαιστος,) Mercury, ('Ερμῆς,) who were masculine deities ; and Juno, ("Ηρα,) Minerva, (Παλλάς,) Venus, ('Αφροδίτη,) Ceres, (Δημήτηρ,) Diana, ("Αρτεμις,) Vesta, ('Εστια,) who were feminine. For these gods, the Greeks had the highest veneration, and at Athens was an altar erected called βομὸς τῶν δώδεκα θεῶν, 'the altar of the twelve gods.'

There were many other divinities of a nature between divine and human, (δαίμονες.) Several men illustrious for their virtues and exploits, were ranked among the gods. The gods of other nations were introduced, and altars erected to them, but this was not allowed without a public decree of the court of the Areopagus. Their divinities were in number, it is supposed, more than three thousand.* Perhaps, however, this may include all the different names which were often applied to the same deity.

In the earliest ages of the world men did not worship in temples, but in the open air, and on the summits of the highest mountains; for as these appeared nearer the heavens, they thought that the gods could more readily hear their supplications. The Greeks early adopted the custom of erecting temples. They were built with the greatest splendor and richest magnificence that art or wealth could produce. They generally faced the east, as the rising sun was an object of adoration.

Temples (ναοί ἱερά) were dedicated to the worship of one divinity or more. The altar (βωμὸς) was of various dimensions, according to the different gods to which it might be consecrated. On the altar the offerings and sacrifices were made. Altars were often erected under the shade of trees in groves. The temples were adorned with statues of the gods, (ἀγαλματα,) and offerings, (ἀναθήματα.) Temples, statues, and altars were esteemed so sacred, that to most of them was granted the

* According to Hesiod, thirty-three thousand.

privilege of protecting offenders, as it was considered sacrilege to force from them any criminals who had fled to them for safety. There were also sacred fields (τεμένη) which were set apart for religious purposes.

The sacred persons (ἱερεῖς, priests) were intrusted with the care of the temples, and other sacred places, and of the religious ceremonies. Being esteemed as the mediators between the gods and men, they were consequently held in the highest veneration. The chief magistrates were frequently consecrated to the priesthood. It was required of all priests that they should be without blemish in their persons and moral character. The high-priests (ἀρχιερεῖς, βασιλεῖς, πρυτάνεις) were ranked the first, for they presided at the celebration of the most sacred mysteries. These had their inferior ministers.

The women were admitted to sacred offices, and were called ἱέρειαι, priestesses. They were generally virgins.

Section II.

Prayers, Sacrifices, Purifications, and Oaths.

At the commencement of any undertaking, individuals addressed their prayers to the gods, which they offered up in the morning, the evening, and at the rising and setting of the sun and moon. Prayers were called εὐχαί, προσευχαί, δεήσεισ, λιταί, &c., and thanksgiving was named εὐχαριστία. The greatest reverence was observed in praying to the gods. The usual posture was that of kneeling, but they occasionally prayed standing, sitting, or wholly prostrate.

In their public solemnities, the Athenians offered their prayers in common, for the prosperity of the state and of their allies, for the fruits of the earth, for rain, or for deliverance from pestilence or famine. The splendor of these ceremonies presented an imposing appearance. The space before the temple and the porticoes that surrounded it were filled with people. The priests assembled around the altar, and recited prayers, after which the sacred hymns were chanted by choruses of youths.

In the early ages of Greece, sacrifices (θυσίαι, δῶρα, ἱερά) were of a very simple kind, and confined to the fruits of the earth. Afterward myrrh, frankincense, and costly offerings were used ; and subsequently animals. The animals usually sacrificed were the ox, the hog, the sheep, the kid, the cock, and the goose. Each deity had his appropriate victim. The animals also differed according to the different classes of the gods : to the infernal and evil deities black victims were offered ; to the good and celestial, white.

The rich were required to make costly sacrifices, but the poor, who were unable to sacrifice animals, offered cakes (πόπανα) of barley-meal. The largest and principal victim offer

ed was the ox. It was required that all the
victims should be sound, and without blemish.

The Spartans performed their sacrifices with
as little display as possible, but the Athenian
priests were very richly attired. The victim was
led to the altar adorned with wreaths and garlands, and sometimes with its horns gilded.
The priests then went round it, and sprinkled
it with holy water, (χέρνιψ,) with which they
often also sprinkled those persons who were
present. They then placed upon its head
cakes made of salt and barley, (οὐλαί,) and
plucked from its forehead, between the horns,
a little hair, which they threw into the fire
upon the altar. The priest then said, Εὐχώμεθα,
'Let us pray.' After prayers, a little wine
was poured upon the head of the victim, and
the altars were strewed with frankincense.
The priest, or his assistant, then knocked the
animal on the head, and cut its throat. If the
animal escaped the blow, or did not fall, or
was a long time in dying, it was deemed un-
acceptable to the gods. The blood of the victim was received in a vessel. The soothsayer
or augur (σπλαγχνοσκόπος) then examined the entrails. Certain parts of the animal were then
sprinkled with barley-meal, and placed upon
the altar to be burned. Wine was often poured upon the flame to make it rise higher.
There were peculiar ceremonies for each deity, but the general plan of the sacrifice was
the same. It was sometimes customary to

dance around the altars, and sing sacred hymns while the sacrifice was burning. The hymns (παιᾶνες) had their particular names, according to the deity in honor of whom they were sung.

After the sacrifice was over, a feast was made, and for that purpose tables were provided in all the temples. The Greeks continued singing throughout the feast, after which games were introduced. These being over, libations (σπονδαί, λοιβαί, χοαι) of wine were offered to Jupiter, and the tongue of the victim was cast into the fire in honor of Mercury, the god of eloquence. Libations of wine were also made upon the commencement of any journey. Other liquids besides wine were used in libations, as water, honey, milk, and oil.

The Greeks never entered upon any religious duty without previously undergoing some process of purification. They always performed this ceremony if they were about to visit the temples, or to offer sacrifices, or to be initiated into any of the sacred mysteries, or to make any vow or prayer to the gods. One method of purification was by washing the hands in a vessel (περιῤῥαντήριον) filled with holy water, and placed at the entrance of the temple. Another method was to draw around the person to be purified a squill or sea-onion, (σκίλλα,) which plant was thought to possess peculiar virtues There was also carried around the person a young dog, (σκύλαξ.) The Greeks also purified themselves after they had committed any act by which they thought themselves polluted, such as murder, attendance at a funeral ; for a dead body was thought to pollute every thing about it. On this account, the house in which the dead had been laid out was purified with fire and sulphur.

The oaths (ὅρκοι) were of two kinds, the great oath and the less oath. The most common oath was Μὰ Δία, ' By Jupiter.' The Greeks swore, however, by other deities, and sometimes by the dead.

In swearing, they raised their hands towards heaven ; in great oaths, they laid them upon the altar. In all private contracts the individuals concerned pledged their faith by taking each other by the right hand. In solemn and important treaties, they sacrificed to the gods, and prayed to them that he who should first violate the conditions of the oath might die in the same manner as the victim just sacrificed. Perjured persons sometimes were punished with death. Yet the Greeks were by other nations charged with perfidy, and the phrase *Græca fides,* ' Grecian faith,' was a proverb applied to inconstant and deceitful persons or nations.

SECTION III.

Divination and Oracles.

The power of prying into futurity, or divination, (μαντική,) was universally accredited among the Greeks. There were several different kinds of divinations. The following were the principal.

1. Divination by appearances in the heavens, such as thunder, lightning, comets, eclipses, and meteors. Thunder or lightning on the right was deemed a good omen; if on the left, a bad one.

2. Divination by the flight and singing of birds, as they were seen or heard on the right or left. If a flock of birds flew about any person, it was esteemed a lucky omen. The hawk, buzzard, swallow, and owl, were considered as unlucky birds. The crowing of the cock was a favorable omen.

3. Divination from beasts, insects, and reptiles. Bees were deemed an omen of future eloquence. Toads were accounted lucky omens, and serpents unlucky. If a timorous animal, as a hare, appeared in time of war, it signified defeat.

4. Divination by sacrifices. If the victim approached the altar reluctantly, or eluded the stroke of the axe, or did not bleed freely, if the entrails were decayed or defective, if the heart was small, the gods were thought to be unpropitious; if otherwise, the omens were good. If the fire was kindled easily, and burned clearly, if the flame immediately consumed the victim, the sacrifice was thought to be acceptable.

5. Divination by dreams or visions, as when gods or spirits conversed with men in their sleep, or the images of things about to happen were presented to their view. Dreams in the early part of the morning were most regarded.

6. Divination by casting lots, as by throwing into vessels white and black beans, which had their characters inscribed upon them or given them before they were thrown; or by drawing pieces of paper from an urn, and reading the prophetic lines written on them.

7. Divination by ominous words and things. The Greeks were careful to avoid the use of ominous words, such as θάνατος, 'death,' for which they often substituted τέλος, 'the end' of life. Palpitations of the heart, ringings in the ears, and sneezing were observed. If the ringing was in the right ear, it was deemed a good omen. To sneeze between midnight and the following noon was esteemed fortunate, but between noon and midnight, unfortunate. All unusual accidents were presages from which future events were inferred.

Of all kinds of divination, oracles (χρησμοί) were held in the highest repute, as they were supposed to proceed directly from the gods. They were consulted in all important affairs. If a form of government was to be altered laws to be enacted, war declared, or peace concluded, the will of the gods was sought by consulting the oracles. No one could consult the oracles without first making rich presents and offering sacrifices to the gods, and this only upon- stated days. Jupiter was the most eminent of all the deities who presided over oracles, and next to him Apollo. The general characteristics of the answers of the oracles were ambiguity, obscurity, and a susceptibility of changing the terms or expressions, so as to apply to various and opposite events.

The oracle of Jupiter at Dodona, a city of Epirus, was much celebrated. At the side of the temple was a forest of oaks, one of which was called the divine or prophetic oak, though all the trees were thought to be gifted with the spirit of prophecy. It is supposed that the priests or priestesses, when they were consulted, ascended one of these oaks, and gave their answers.

The oracle of Trophonius in Bœotia was in great reputation. After many preliminary ceremonies, such as washing, offering sacrifices, drinking from the fountain of Lethe, the votaries went down into a cave, (at night only,) by means of small ladders. At the bottom was another little cavern, of which the entrance was very small. Their feet were placed within the opening of the little cave, which was no sooner done, than they perceived themselves borne into it with great force and velocity. They were required to carry with them cakes made of honey in each hand. Futurity was revealed to them in frightful voices and

terrific appearances, and they generally returned quite stupified.

But the most celebrated of all the Grecian
oracles was that of Apollo at Delphi. ˆ He
was worshipped there under the name of the
Pythian, from the serpent Python, which he
had there killed. Delphi stood upon a declivity about the middle of mount Parnassus. On
the declivity of the hill was discovered a cavern, from which issued a strong sulphurous
vapor, producing a kind of intoxication of the
brain of those who approached it. The persons under the influence of this phrensy would
utter incoherent sounds and words which were
supposed to foretell futurity. A priestess was
appointed, called Πυϑία, to receive the inspira-
tion from the cavern, and thence give her oracles. A temple was erected, which became a
most costly and magnificent building. It was
surrounded with statues and the richest works
of art, and was filled with the most costly
presents to the god, which were brought from
every part of the world. At first a single
priestess sufficed to answer to those who came
to consult the oracle, but afterwards there were
two others appointed.

Over the vent, from whence issued the prophetic exhalation, was placed a tripod, upon
which the Pythian sat and gave her responses.
She could not prophecy till she was intoxicated
by the vapor from the sanctuary. The mo-
ment she was seated upon the tripod, the di-

vine vapor began to produce the most singular
and violent effects upon her. Her eyes rolled
wildly, her hair stood erect, her whole frame
was convulsed, and she uttered the wildest
and most incoherent cries. It was the few
words that she thus uttered, that the priests
carefully collected, and afterwards delivered
to those who came to consult the oracle. The
reputation of this oracle almost effaced that
of all others.

There were oracles in all parts of Greece,
but the three which have been noticed were
the most eminent.

SECTION IV.

Grecian Festivals.

The Festivals of the Greeks were acts of
religion, since they were instituted in honor of
the gods to avert some evil, or obtain some
good, or to return thanks to them for some
blessings conferred. There were also festivals
in honor of illustrious men. An infinite number of these feasts were celebrated in the several cities of Greece, and especially at Athens.

The Panathenea (Παναθήναια) was celebrated
at Athens in honor of Minerva, the tutelary
goddess of that city. It was at first called
from her name, Athenia, but after Theseus

had united the several towns of Attica into one city, it took the name of Panathenea. These feasts were of two kinds, the great and the less, which were observed with almost the same ceremonies, the less annually, and the great, upon the expiration of every fourth year, and with greater pomp and magnificence than the less. In these feasts were exhibited races, gymnastic exercises, and combats, and contention for the prizes of music and poetry. Whoever obtained the victory in any of the games of this festival was rewarded with a vessel of oil, and a crown of olives. This feast continued several days.

The Dionysia (Διονύσια) were festivals in honor of Bacchus, (Διόνυσος.) They were also called ὄργια, from the fury (ὀργή) of the Bacchanalians. In these feasts the public were entertained with games, shows, and dramatic representations, which were attended by a vast concourse of people. At the same time the poets disputed for the prize of poetry.

These feasts continued many days. Those who attended, mimicked whatever the poets had thought to feign of the god Bacchus. Men and women ridiculously transformed themselves, by putting on the skins of wild beasts; and in this manner appeared night and day in public, imitating drunkenness, and dancing in most indecent postures, screaming and howling furiously, Ἐυοῖ Βάκχε and Ἰώ Βάκχε. There were two kinds of these festivals, the greater and

X

the less ; the former celebrated in the city, the latter in the country.

There is nothing in all Pagan antiquity more celebrated than the feasts of Ceres, at Eleusis, hence called the Eleusinian Mysteries, ('Ελευσίνια,) which were celebrated every fifth year by the Athenians, and were of nine days continuance.

The temple in which the ceremonies of ini tiation were performed was constructed of the best quality of Pentelic marble, and in a most magnificent manner. None but the initiated were permitted on any pretence to enter the temple. The priest who initiated persons into the mysteries of the greater feast was called 'Ιεροφάντης, 'a revealer of holy things.' The ceremony of initiation was performed at night. What these mysteries or secrets were, is not fully known, as all were bound by an oath not to reveal them. It is very generally agreed that they were subservient to the cause of vir- tue and religion. The character of every ap- plicant for initiation was carefully examined, and a whole year was devoted to this purpose. During the festival it was unlawful to seize criminals or commence any lawsuit. Various games, combats, processions, and amusements were solemnized during the feast.

There were numerous other festivals, but all of minor importance.

CHAPTER VI.

GAMES AND AMUSEMENTS OF THE GREEKS.

SECTION I.

Athletic Exercises.

THERE were five principal exercises practised in the Grecian games, viz.: Running
races on foot and on horse, (δρόμος;) Leaping,
(ἄλμα;) Boxing, (πυγμή;) Wrestling, (πάλη;)
and throwing the Discus or Quoit, (δίσκος.) The
general name of Athletæ (ἀθληταί) was given
to those who exercised themselves with a design to dispute the prizes in the public games.

Of all the exercises which the Athletæ cultivated, running was in the highest estimation.
The place where they exercised themselves
was called the stadium, (στάδιον.) The runners
or racers, upon the signal being given, rushed
forward to the goal (τέλος, τέρμα, σκοπός) with
their greatest swiftness, and he who first reached it, received a prize, (ἄθλον, βραβεῖον.)

There were also horse races, and chariot-
races. These latter were in high renown.

The skill of the charioteer was exhibited in turning the boundary or goals, (νύσσαι,) by keeping as near it as possible, and yet avoiding it.

Leaping was sometimes performed with the hands empty, and at other times with weights of lead or stone, which were thrown forward by the motions of the arms in jumping, and thus enabled the Athletæ to leap further than they could without them.

In boxing, the combatants covered their fists with a kind of offensive arms, called cestus, (ἱμάς,) which was a glove made of straps of leather and plated inside with brass, lead, or iron. Their use was to strengthen the hands of the combatants, and to add violence to the blows. Boxing was one of the most dangerous of the gymnastic combats, because, beside the liability of being crippled, the combatants ran the hazard of their lives. Seldom did one gain a victory without paying for it with the loss of an eye, or the severe maiming of some part of the body. He who yielded the victory to his antagonist, acknowledged his defeat either by his voice, by letting his arms fall, or by sinking to the ground.

Wrestling was at first practised with little art, but afterward more address and skill were employed. The wrestlers, before they began the combat, anointed their bodies with oil to give flexibility to their limbs; and then rolled themselves in the dust to prevent the skin from being too slippery. Several matches contended at the same time. To obtain the victory it was necessary for one to throw his adversary twice, and to renew the combat three times. The Pancratium (πανκράτιον) was a contest which included both boxing and wrestling. The Pancratiast was allowed to gain the victory over his adversary in any manner, as by scratching, biting, kicking, together with any artifice of boxing or wrestling.

The Discus or Quoit was of a round form, made sometimes of wood, but more frequently of stone, lead, iron, or brass. It had a hole in the centre, through which was put a thong, by means of which it was thrown. This exercise was a trial of bodily strength more than of skill. The Athletæ did not endeavor to strike a given mark with the discus, but to throw beyond their competitors. They all used the same discus, and he who threw it farthest was the victor.

Section II.

The Games, Olympic, Pythian, Nemean, and Isthmian.

There were four kinds of games solemnized in Greece ;—the Olympic, the Pythian, the Nemean, and the Isthmian. These differed from each other chiefly in the places where they were celebrated; the ceremonies and exercises in each being nearly the same.

Amongst all these games, the Olympic held the first rank, and that for three reasons:—They were sacred to Jupiter, the greatest of the gods;—instituted by Hercules, the first of heroes;—and celebrated with more pomp and magnificence, amidst a greater assemblage of spectators from all parts, than any of the rest of the games. They were celebrated at Olympia, a town of Elis, in Peloponnesus, after the expiration of every four years; and continued five days. It was not permitted for any woman to be present except the priestesses of Ceres, upon pain of death; for at many of the exercises the combatants fought naked. The ceremonies of these games commenced with sacrifices on the night preceding the first day; and at day-break the games commenced. These continued during the five days of the celebration; and were those noticed in the preceding section. Judges were appointed to preside over the games, to award the prizes, and to punish with scourging all who were guilty of any irregularity or unfairness. The moral character of those who were about to engage as combatants was carefully examined.

These games were not devoted exclusively to contests of physical power. They were intellectual as well as gymnastic festivals. The poets, orators, and historians here recited their productions; and in the presence of the whole assemblage had the prizes awarded to them.

.The Greeks thought nothing comparable to the victory in these games. They looked upon it as the perfection of glory, and did not believe that mortals could desire any thing beyond it. In the Olympic games the reward ot the victor was a simple wreath of wild olive. He was also carried home in a triumphal chariot, and sometimes the honor was paid to him of dating the year with his name.

The influence of these games upon the character of the Greeks was very beneficial. In training themselves for these severe exercises, they were preparing for the hardships and contests of war. In no way, however, were the games more decidedly beneficial than in encouraging a literary spirit and in diffusing literary information. The most distinguished authors of Greece obtained prizes at Olympia, for excelling in contests of mental power.

The Olympic games were established about 776 years before Christ, from which period the Olympiads are reckoned.

The Pythian games were celebrated in honor of Apollo, at Delphi; and were at first held every nine years, and consisted only of musical contests; but afterward they were observed every five years, and were solemnized with the same exercises and contests which were practised in the Olympic games. Songs,

dances, and musical instruments were introduced. The prizes were garlands of laurel.

The Nemean games received their name
from Nemea, a city and sacred grove of Argolis. They were celebrated every third year,
or more properly on the first and third year of
every Olympiad. The exercises were principally the same as in the other games; and the
victors were at first crowned with a wreath of
olive, but afterwards with parsley.

The Isthmian games received the name from
the Isthmus of Corinth, where they were celebrated. They were consecrated to Neptune.
They were solemnized every three years. The
prize at first was a crown of pine, afterwards
of dry parsley; and again the pine was restored. The inhabitants of Elis were the only
people of Greece who were not admitted to
these games, in consequence of a dreadful ex-
ecration denounced against them if they ever
should be present.

Section III.

The Theatre and Drama.

There were many tragic and comic poets
before Thespis, but as he was the first that
made any improvements in the poem and its
manner of representation, he is generally

considered the inventor of the Grecian Drama, and the founder of the Grecian Theatre. But Æschylus was the founder of a fixed and durable theatre, adorned with suitable decorations. It was first built of wood, but afterward the most superb and magnificent structures were erected.

The theatre was divided into three principal parts :—1. The stage or scene, (λογεῖον, σκηνή,) where the actors stood during the performances, and where were represented paintings, and objects that corresponded with the piece performed. 2. The orchestra, (ὀρχήστρα,) the place assigned for pantomimes, dancers, and the chorus. 3. The theatre, (θέατρον,) where the spectators sat. This last must have been of vast extent, as at Athens it was capable of containing above thirty thousand persons. The theatre was of a semicircular form. The space contained within the semicircle was allotted to the spectators, and had seats placed, one above another, to the top of the building. In front of the spectators was the orchestra, and still farther in front was the stage and scene.

The great theatres had three rows of porticoes erected one upon another, which formed the body of the edifice ; and three different stories for the seats. The theatres were all open above, and the plays were always represented in daylight, and in the open air.

The number of actors (ὑποκριταί) which appeared on the stage at any one time was three. As a body of men; the actors were dissolute in habits and morals; yet there were some honorable exceptions.

The fondness for theatrical representations was no doubt one of the principal causes of the degeneracy, corruption, and decline of the Athenian republic.

The progress of the drama was regular, but slow. Æschylus gave a new form to tragedy, both in its representation, and in its style and spirit; and is often on this account esteemed the founder of Grecian tragedy.

CHAPTER VII.

DOMESTIC AFFAIRS OF THE GREEKS.

Section I.

Dwellings, Furniture, &c.

THE houses (ὄικοι) of the Greeks were, in general, small and mean, though some individuals erected, as private dwellings, edifices which almost rivalled the temples in cost and magnificence. They were built of stone, wood, and unburnt bricks dried in the air. There was sometimes a small court-yard in front; but usually they were built directly upon the street, having their upper stories projecting somewhat, and their stair-case (κγίμαξ) upon the outside. The doors (θύρα and πύλη) were hung upon wooden posts, (παραστάδες,) and over these were suspended small bells. The men and women had distinct apartments, in every house, assigned them.

Amongst the furniture of the Greeks was the δίφρος, 'a settee;' θρόνος, 'a chair;' κλισμός, 'a sofa;' θρῆνυς, 'a footstool;' κλίναι, 'couches;' and τράπεζα, 'a table.'

Besides the public baths, which at Athens were very numerous, most of the more wealthy citizens had private baths in their own houses

There was a difference between δίκίαι and συνοικίαι, the former meaning 'dwelling-houses,' which were occupied by one family; and the latter, 'lodging-houses,' which were rented for lodgings to several families.

SECTION II.

Dress of the Greeks.

Among the ancient Greeks, the men had no coverings for their heads. They afterwards wore hats, (πῖλοι.) The head-dress of the women consisted of the veil, (κάλυπτρα;) a fillet, (ἄμπυξ,) with which the hair was tied; a veil, (κρήδεμνον,) which came down upon the shoulders; a net, (κεκρύφαλος,) in which the hair was enclosed; and a mitre or turban, (μίτρα.) Earrings (ἕρματα) and necklaces (ὅρμοι) were common.

The inner garment both of men and women was the tunic, (χιτών.) The tunic of the men descended to the knees, that of the women to their feet. Over the tunic they threw a mantle. The exterior garment was the cloak or mantle, (ἱμάτιον,) which was a large piece of woollen cloth, nearly square, which was wrapped around the body, or fastened about the shoulders; and served also to wrap themselves in at night. The χλαῖνα was a thicker external robe, used in cold weather. The λῆδος was a light garment, worn in the summer. The τριβων was the cloak of philosophers and poor persons, and was made of very coarse material. The στολή was a long robe that reached to the feet. The χλαμύς was a military cloak. The ψέλλια were bracelets with which the hands and arms of the women were decorated.

The shoes (ὑποδήματα) were of many kinds. They were tied under the soles of the feet with thongs or cords, (ἱμάντες.)

Among the Athenians, the quality of the dress differed according to the age, family, rank, means, and taste of the wearer. Woollen garments were the most common, though linen ones were worn, especially by women; and were at a low price, except the finest kinds.

The Spartans had a uniform dress, which they preserved for many ages. Their milita ry costume was of a red color.

The Greeks in general set a high value on scarlet color, and a still greater on purple.

The Athenians often wore in their hair golden grasshoppers, called τέττιγες, as emblems of the antiquity of their nation, intimating that they were sprung from the earth, as they supposed the grasshoppers were.

SECTION III.

Marriage Customs, and Condition of Females in Greece.

Marriage was regarded, in all the different states of Greece, as a most honorable state of life, and received great encouragement by legal regulations. Celibacy was considered a very great reproach, and in some communities was attended with the infliction of punishment by law. The Lacedæmonians, particularly, were very severe towards those who deferred to marry, or who abstained from it altogether. No Spartan could live unmarried beyond the time prescribed by the laws, without incurring various penalties. At Athens no man could hold any public office, or even plead any public cause, unless he were married, and had children, and estates in land, for these were considered as so many pledges for his good conduct.

At Sparta, the usual age for men to marry was thirty, and for women, twenty years. The Athenians had a law prohibiting men from marrying before the age of thirty-five.

It was highly disgraceful to marry within certain degrees of relationship. The Spartans were not permitted to marry any of their kindred. Citizens were forbidden to marry only with citizens. The consent of the parents was necessary; for parental authority in this age was absolute.

The custom for the wife to bring a dowry (προιξ φερνή) to her husband, was common in nearly all the states of Greece, except in Sparta. When maidens, who were the daughters of those who had been serviceable to their country, had no relations to assist them, the state gave them a portion from the public treasury as a dowry.

Before the solemnization of the marriage, it was necessary to offer sacrifices to the gods of marriage, and if any unlucky omen appeared, the contract was dissolved, and the marriage prevented. The maiden also propitiated the virgin goddess Diana (who was averse to marriage) by presents. The bride and her retinue were dressed in the richest manner. The bridegroom generally came to the house of the bride in a chariot, and conducted her to the temple where the rites were to be performed. Many persons preceded and followed the chariot, singing the praises of the happy pair, and of the gods of marriage. They were received at the temple by the priest, who led them to the altar, where sacrifices were offered to Diana. If these were favorable, the father or guardian of the bride took her by the hand and presented her to the bridegroom. The parties then swore inviolable fidelity to each other, and their parents ratified the oaths by new sacrifices. These ceremonies were performed in the latter part of the day, so that the night came on before they left the temple. A procession then preceded the newly-married pair, carrying torches and attended by a band of musicians, and conducted them to the house of the husband, which was hung with garlands, and splendidly illuminated. A sumptuous feast was provided, and while they were enjoying the repast, they were entertained with bands of singers and dancers around the house.

The marriage ceremonies of the Spartans were different from those of all the other Grecian states. Instead of any public celebration, every thing was done as privately as possible. When every thing had been settled between the parties, the bridegroom went secretly to the house of his bride, and carried her off by night. Before day he returned to his companions at the Gymnasia ; and seldom visited his wife in the day time ; for it was considered as unmanly to acknowledge the influence of love, or any other passion, except patriotism.

The condition of women in Greece, even in the ages of the most refinement and civilization, was degraded. They performed every servile duty for their husbands, such as drawing water, feeding the cattle, harnessing and unharnessing the horses in the chariots, &c. Their education, too, was extremely limited, seldom knowing how to read or write. They were considered as the slaves, rather than the companions of men ; they were not permitted to mingle in his society, and were confined to a particular quarter of the house. From most of the public games and amusements they were rigidly excluded. The Spartan women, however, were not under the same restraint as those of other parts of Greece.

Section IV.

Education of Children.

Though the education of children, and especially of the males, was not neglected in any of the states of Greece, yet in Athens there was far more attention paid to it than in

the rest of the states. The names of the
Athenian children were inscribed in the public registers soon after their birth. On the
seventh or tenth day they were named; on
which occasion sacrifices were offered. For
the first five years no labor of any kind was
imposed upon them, and they were left free
from all restraint of dress, that they might acquire an easy and graceful movement, and a
vigorous constitution. The male children were
very early taught to swim, which was considered an important attainment in a country
where every citizen was liable to be called to
serve in the navy. At the age of seven they
were enrolled in the register of the tribe to
which their parents belonged, and were then
placed under the superintendence of private
teachers, (παιδαγωγοί,) and the directors of the
Gymnasia, (παιδοτρίβαι.) By the former, their
minds were stored with virtuous principles,
and with the knowledge of the arts and sciences; and by the latter, they were inured to
hunger and thirst, heat and cold, fatigue and
hardships. They were exercised in throwing
the javelin, to manage the most spirited horses,
to wrestle and box, to run, throw the discus,
&c. These exercises were intended to prepare them for war.

A portion of the day was required to be devoted in attendance upon the instructions of
the grammarians, (γραμματισταί,) where they
were taught 'letters,' which term comprehend
Y

ed history, poetry, eloquence, and literature in general. The most scrupulous attention was paid to pronunciation. They were instructed in Arithmetic, Geography, Geometry, Tactics, Natural Science, and Morals. These various branches were taught by professors, who established schools for themselves respectively, in some department of literature in which they considered themselves most proficient.

Section V.

Manners and Customs in Private Life.

The Greeks, as well as most of the nations of antiquity, were accustomed to rise early. At Athens, they usually rose at day-break, and after a few short devotional exercises, entered upon the employments of the day. As their habits of living were plain, and the necessaries of life procured without money or labor, the Athenians had a great deal of leisure time. This they spent in various exercises and amusements, such as hunting, walking, frequenting the Gymnasia or Baths. Their habits in later times were not so free from luxury.

The Spartans looked with contempt on the festivals, public shows, and other amusements of the Athenians. The cultivation of the social affections was at Sparta disregarded and considered as effeminate. The diet was coarse, and the meals eaten at public tables. Ornament had no part in the dress of the Spartan. They paid great reverence to age.

The food (ὄψον) of the Greeks consisted more of vegetable than animal substances. The principal kinds of bread were maize-bread (ἄρτος) and barley-bread, (μάζα.) There were cakes made of various ingredients. Salt was used in every article of food, and in great abundance. `·`

The common beverage was water. When wine was used it was always diluted with water; the usual proportions being two parts of wine to two parts of water. To drink to excess was very disgraceful, and he who committed a crime when intoxicated was more severely punished than if he had committed it when sober.

The times of eating were four every day. 1. The morning meal, or breakfast, (ἀκράτισμα, ἄριστον,) which was taken about the rising of the sun;—2. The meal at noon, or dinner, (δεῖπνον;) 3. The afternoon meal, (δείλινόν;) 4. The evening meal or supper, (δόρπος,) which was afterwards called δεῖπνον. Dinner was a short, plain meal; and the supper, taken about sunset, was the principal meal of the Greeks

There were several kinds of entertainments among the Greeks, such as the marriage feast, (γάμος.) and the club feast, (ἔρανος,) in which latter, every one contributed his portion. There were also city-feasts and tribe-feasts. Before the Greeks went to a convivial entertainment, they washed and anointed themselves, and those who came from a distance were washed and clothed in the house of the entertainer (ἑστιάτωρ) before they were admitted to the feast. It was also customary to wash between the courses, and then again after supper. At their private meals, the Greeks sometimes sat, but at the entertainments, they always reclined on couches, leaning on their left arm.

Before they commenced eating, they made an offering to the gods of some of their provisions. When the entertainment was finished, a libation of wine with a prayer was offered, and a hymn sung to the gods. Music and dancing were introduced, and then various other exercises and amusements.

Section VI.

Occupations, Arts, and Sciences.

The Grecians usually attended but to one employment, whether it were civil, agricultural, commercial, or mechanical. The inhabitants of the country were devoted to agriculture, and those of the city to commerce and manufactures. As their habits of living were

simple, their wants were the more easily supplied; and hence all had much leisure time
for amusements, or acquiring knowledge. In
the useful and necessary arts, the Greeks never
made any great improvement. But in the
fine arts, Greece was superior to all ancient
nations, and probably excelled by no modern.
They carried architecture, sculpture, and
painting to such a state of perfection, that
little room is left for improvement by the
moderns. Their architecture (ἀρχιτεκτονικὴ) consisted of three distinct orders, the Doric, the
Ionic, and the Corinthian. The Doric possessed a masculine grandeur and sublime simpli-
city. The Ionic was marked with graceful-
ness and elegance. The Corinthian affected
the highest magnificence and ornament, by
uniting the characteristics of the other orders.

In sculpture (γλυφὴ) the Greeks excelled no
less than in architecture. Specimens of their
skill in this art are considered perfect models.

In painting, (γραφικὴ,) though but few specimens have reached us, they are supposed also
to have greatly excelled, as the productions of
their celebrated painters were highly extolled
by the writers of antiquity. Painting was
considered an elegant accomplishment, and
the sons of the richest citizens generally devoted much time to it.

In music (μουσικὴ) the Greeks were celebrated, but they appear to have been less versed
in this branch of the fine arts, than several

modern nations. It was deemed an indispensable branch of education among the Athenians. With the Spartans, also, music was a favorite amusement, but it was entirely of a martial kind. But at Athens every species of music was cultivated to a high degree. There were seven notes, and four modes, (νόμοι,)—the Phrygian, which was religious or sacred; the Doric, which was martial; the Lydian, which was sad and plaintive; and the Ionic, which was gay, lively, and brilliant, and used upon festive occasions. In their instrumental music they used principally the lyre, (κιθάρα,) the flute, (αὐλός,) and the pipe, (σύριγξ.)

In writing (γραφή) they generally used black ink, (μέλαν γραφικόν.) Their paper (χαρτης) was made from several materials, as from the skins of beasts, bark of trees, and from the Egyptian *papyrus*, which was a kind of flag.* The pen or stylus (στύλος) was made of iron, ivory, reeds, or quills.

In science and literature, Greece was the glory of the whole earth. Poetry, Oratory, History, and Philosophy were cultivated among them in the highest degree. Their philosophy was, however, merely speculative, and seldom based upon facts.

* See Roman Antiquities, Chap. vi., Sect. vi.

Section VII.

Treatment of the Dead.   Funeral Rites, &c.

The funerals of the Greeks were attended with many ceremonies, showing that they considered the duties belonging to the dead to be of the highest importance.   In their opinion it was the most awful of all imprecations to wish that a person might die without the honor of burial ; and of all kinds of death, that by shipwreck was deemed the most terrible, since the body was not then interred.   The reason why they were so religiously solicitous respecting the interment of the departed was, in consequence of their firm belief that their spirits or souls could not be admitted into the Elysian fields, but would wander desolate and wretched upon the banks of the river Styx, till their bodies were deposited in the earth.

When any person was thought to be dangerously ill, they placed over his door branches of buckthorn and laurel—the former to ward off evil ; and the latter to render Apollo, the god of medicine, propitious.   When he appeared at the point of death, it was customary for his relations and friends to assemble around his bed, to kiss and embrace him, to bid him farewell, and to catch his dying words, which they ever after repeated with the greatest reverence.   As soon as he had expired, they beat brazen kettles, by which they designed to drive away evil spirits, and to secure his soul from the Furies. The relations closed his eyes and mouth, covered his face, washed his body, anointed it with oil, wrapped it in linen cloth, decked it with garlands of flowers, and laid it out at the entrance of the house, that all might readily see it. Before interment, a piece of money was put into the mouth of the corpse, generally an *obolus*, which was to be Charon's fare for ferrying the departed spirit across the Styx. A cake of flour and honey was also put into his mouth, to appease the fury of the dog Cerberus, who guarded the entrance of the place of departed spirits.

The usual time of burial was on the third or fourth day after death. The funeral ceremony was performed in the daytime, but it was customary to carry lighted torches at all burials. The procession was generally on horseback or in carriages; but at the funerals of distinguished personages the company went on foot, which was thought to show more respect. The relations went next to the corpse.

The custom of burning the dead was common among the Greeks. When the funeral pile (πυρά) upon which the body was consumed was burnt down, they extinguished the fire with wine, and collected the bones and ashes. These they deposited in urns, (χάλπαι, &c.,) which they buried.

The Greeks expressed their sorrow for the

dead in various modes of mourning, such as, abstaining from feasts and entertainments, banishing from their houses all musical instruments, absenting themselves from society, divesting themselves of all ornaments, jewels, &c., putting on mourning garments of black and coarse materials, shaving off their hair, sprinkling ashes upon their heads, walking softly, to express faintness and loss of strength, beating their breasts, accusing the gods.

The dead were sometimes buried in temples, but usually in the public burial-places without the city walls, by the side of the highways. The Spartans, however, buried their dead usually within the city. Tombstones were polished and adorned with great art. The monuments of various kinds were called by the general name μνημεῖα. A cenotaph (κενοτάφια) was an empty monument erected to such as had been buried in another place, or to such as had perished without any burial. To deface a sepulchre was a most sacrilegious crime.

There were various honors paid to the dead, such as funeral orations, games, repasts, sacrifices, and libations. Most of the honors were paid on the ninth day after the funeral, and also on the thirtieth.

z

CHAPTER VIII.

TIME, MEASURES, WEIGHTS, AND MONEY OF THE GREEKS.

Section I.

Divisions of Time.

The Grecians computed time in years, (ἔτη,) months, (μῆνες,) and days, (ἡμέραι.) The year of the Athenians began on the first new moon after the summer solstice, which now takes place on the 21st of June. Their year was divided into twelve months, each of which contained thirty and twenty-nine days alternately. The time thus lost, by using the lunar instead of the solar year, was made up by inserting intercalary months in different years. Their year beginning in the last part of June, their first month comprised the greater part of July, which month is usually considered as their first month.

The names of their months were—1. Ἑκατομβαιών, 'July ;'—2. Μεταγειτνιών, 'August ;'—3. Βοηδρομιών, 'September ;'—4. Πυανεψιών, 'October;'—5. Μαιμακτηριών, 'November;'—6. Ποσειδεών, 'December;'—7. Γαμηλιών, 'January;'—8. 'Ανθεστηριών, 'February;'—9. 'Ελαφηβολιών, 'March;'—10. Μουνυχιών, 'April;'—11. Θαργηλιών, 'May;'—12. Σκιρροφοριών, 'June.'

Every month was divided into three parts, called decades of days, (δεχήμερα,) and their days named from these, as the first, second, &c., day of the 'decade of the beginning,' 'decade of the middle,' or 'decade of the end.'

An Olympiad was a period of four years, at the end of which the Olympic games were celebrated. The first Olympiad, or rather the first year of the first Olympiad, was 776 years before Christ. To ascertain to what year of the Christian era any given Olympiad corresponds—Subtract 1 from the given Olympiad, multiply the remainder by 4, and add to the product the year of the given Olympiad, and from this sum subtract 1, and the remainder taken from 776, will be the corresponding year of our era. Thus, the 3d of the 31st Olympiad would be B. C. 654 years.

SECTION II.

Dry Measures, Measures of Length, and Weights.

The principal dry measures were the ξέστης, xestes;' the χοῖνιξ, 'chœnix;' and the μέδιμνος,

'medimnus.' The Medimnus contained 1 bush
el, 3 gallons, 5 3-4th pints, or about a bushel
and a half. The Chœnix contained 1 15-16th
pints, or nearly a quart. The Xestes held
about a pint. The Cotyle (κοτύλη) held half a
pint.

The measures of length were—

		Yards	Ft.	Inches.
Δάκτυλος, 'the digit,' . . .				3-4ths.
Πυγμή, 'the cubit,' : . .			1	1 3-5ths.
Πῆχυς, 'the larger cubit,' . .			1	6 1-8th.
'Οργυιά, 'the pace,' . . .			6	0 1-2
Μίλιον, 'the mile,' . .		1611	2	0

The stadium (στάδιον) was nearly equal to an
English furlong, or 201 1-3d yards.

The Grecian foot (ποῦς) was nearly equal to
an English foot, or 1 foot and 7-8ths of an inch.

The Parasang (παρασάγγης) was a Persian
measure equal to about 3 1-2 English miles.

The Plethron (πλέθρον) was a measure of
land about 9-40ths of an English acre. The
Aroura (ἄρουρα) was half a Plethron.

The Grecian weights, reduced to English
Troy weights, were—

	lbs.	oz.	dwt.	grs.
Δραχμή, 'the drachma,' . .			2	16 9-10ths.
Μνᾶ, 'the mina,' or 100 drachmæ,	1	1	10	10
Τάλαντον, 'the talent,' or 60 minæ,	67	7	5	0

The obolus (ὀβολός) was 1-6th of a drachma,
and the chalcus (χαλκός) 1-6th of an obolus.

SECTION III.

Grecian Money.

The coin at Athens was noted for its purity, being entirely free from alloy. The interest of money at Athens varied, according to the degree of risk, from twelve to thirty per cent. Banks, founded on nearly the same principles as those of modern times, were established in Athens.

The coins of Greece, reduced to Federal money, were—

			Dolls.	cts.	mills.
Λεπτόν, 'the lepton,'	(of brass,)	.			1-2
Χαλκός, 'the chalcus,'	"	.		3	1-4th
'Οβολός, 'the obolus,'	"	.		2	7 5-6ths.
Δραχμή, 'the drachma,'	(of silver,)	.		16	6 2-3ds.
Μνᾶ, 'the mina,'	.	. . .	16	66	6 2-3ds.
Τάλαντον, 'the talent,'	.	. .	1000	00	0

Στατήρ, 'the stater,' was a silver and gold coin equivalent to about $4.62 1-2. There were other coins of this name, such as the Stater Daricus, Stater Crœsi, Stater Philippi, &c., which were gold Asiatic coins, and varied in value from $4 to $7 each.

MYTHOLOGY.

It is observable that in all ages and countries, the several nations of the world, however different in their characters, institutions, and manners, have always united in one essential point—the innate opinion of a worship and adoration due to a Supreme Being. Into whatever region we cast our eyes, we find priests, altars, sacrifices, festivals, religious rites, temples, or places consecrated to religious worship. In every race of people we may discover a reverence for the divinity, and homage and worship rendered to him, and an undisguised profession of an entire dependence upon him in all their undertakings, and occasions of need, adversity, or danger. But mere human reason is utterly unable to attain to any certain knowledge of the will, law, or attributes of the Supreme Being. For this, a divine revelation is necessary, and such a revelation only the Jews and Christians have ever possessed. The ideas of the ancients respecting the nature and worship of God were therefore dark, confused, and very imperfect. Their whole religious belief, flowing through the uncertain channel of tradition, and with such embellishments as poetic genius could invent, became more and more corrupt ; and the grossest polytheism and idolatry prevailed among all ancient heathen nations.

The Greeks and Romans worshipped a multiplicity of Gods, celestial, aërial, terrestrial, and infernal, but these were generally divided into three classes ;—celestial, marine, and infernal. All the gods and demi-gods were subject to Jupiter, who was considered the supreme deity of these nations.

The Mythology of the Greeks and Romans is a very extensive subject, and it is only intended here to give a general sketch.

The celestial deities were, Jupiter, Apollo Mars, Mercury, Bacchus, Vulcan, Juno, Minerva, Venus, Diana, Ceres, and Vesta.

JUPITER, the king of gods and men, was the son of Saturn and Rhea or Ops, and born at the same time with Juno, on mount Ida, in Crete. He dethroned his father, and divided his kingdom with his brothers, Neptune and Pluto. Neptune had the dominion of the sea assigned to him, and Pluto that of the infernal regions. The sovereignty of heaven and earth Jupiter reserved for himself.

One of his great exploits was the conquest of the Titans or giants, who heaped mountains upon mountains for the purpose of scaling heaven. He was guilty of indulging in the basest lusts, although he is generally represented as the father of gods and men, as shaking heaven and earth with his nod, and governing all things, except the Fates, by his supreme power.

He is usually represented as sitting on an ivory throne, holding a sceptre in his left hand and a thunderbolt in his right, with an eagle at his feet; and Hebe, the daughter of Juno, and goddess of youth, or the boy Ganymedes, the son of Tros, his cup-bearer, attending him.

APOLLO, the son of Jupiter and Latona, born in the island of Delos, was the god of poetry, music, medicine, divination, the fine arts, and archery. He was also called Phœbus or Sol. He had many oracles, and was called by various names from the places where he was worshipped. For his offence in killing the Cyclops, he was banished from heaven, and obliged to hire himself as a shepherd to Admetus, king of Thessaly; in which occupation he remained nine years.

He is represented as a tall, beardless youth, with long hair, holding a bow and arrows in his right hand, and in his left a lyre or harp. He is crowned with laurel, which was sacred to him, as were the hawk and raven among birds.

MARS, the son of Juno, was the god of war, and patron of all that is bloody and cruel. The most ravenous animals were sacred to him. He is represented as an old man, of a fierce aspect, armed with a spear, riding in a char-

iot drawn by two horses called Flight and Terror, with his sister Bellona for his charioteer.

MERCURY, the son of Jupiter and Mai, was
the messenger of the gods, the patron of travellers, shepherds, orators, merchants, thieves,
and all dishonesty. His exploits* abundant-
ly support his character. He is represented
as a beardless youth, having a winged cap
(*Petasus*) on his head, winged sandals (*Tala-
ria*) on his feet, and a rod or wand (*Caduceus*)
with two serpents bound round it in one hand,
and in the other a purse.

BACCHUS, the son of Jupiter and Semele,
was the god of wine and hilarity. He is represented always young, corpulent, and ruddy,
crowned with vine or ivy leaves, holding in
his hand a *thyrsus*, or spear, bound with ivy,
his chariot drawn by lions or lynxes, attended
by Bacchanals and Satyrs.

VULCAN, the son of Jupiter and Juno, and
husband of Venus, was the god of fire, and of
those who wrought in the metallic arts. He
was kicked out of heaven by Jupiter for at-
tempting to deliver his mother from a chain
by which she was suspended. He continued
to descend nine days and nights, and alighted
on the island of Lemnos; but was crippled
ever after. On this island he had his work-
shop, and also in a cave of Mount Ætna. His

* For the exploits and a minute description of the various
deities, the reader is referred to some Classical Dictionary,
or larger works on Mythology.

workmen were the *Cyclopes,* giants with one eye in their forehead, who were usually employed in making thunderbolts for Jupiter. Vulcan is usually represented as a lame blacksmith, working at his forge, one hand raising a hammer, the other holding a thunderbolt with pincers on an anvil. An eagle waits to carry it to Jupiter when finished.

Juno, the sister and wife of Jupiter, was the queen of the gods, and the goddess of marriage and child-birth. She was born at Argos, or, according to some, at Samos. She was haughty, imperious, and extremely jealous, yet she was held by the ancients in the highest veneration, and there was no other deity, except Apollo, whose worship was more solemn or extensive.

She is represented in a long robe, and magnificent dress, sitting or standing in a light chariot drawn by peacocks, attended by the *Auræ,* or air-nymphs, and by Iris, the goddess of the rainbow. A golden sceptre is usually in her hand, and a diadem adorned with jewels on her head.

Minerva or Pallas, the goddess of wisdom, is said to have sprung completely armed from the brain of Jupiter, by the stroke of Vulcan. She was the most accomplished of all the goddesses, and her worship was universally established, but at Athens, (which received its name from her,) she was especially worshipped. She was the patroness of ship-building, navigation, of war, and of all the useful sciences and arts, such as weaving, spinning, &c.

She is represented as a majestic female, completely armed, of a commanding aspect, bearing a golden breast-plate, a spear in her right hand, and her shield (called *ægis*) in her left, having on it the head of the Gorgon *Medusa*, whose hair was serpents. Her helmet was crowned with olives, and at her feet was an owl or cock.

VENUS, the goddess of love and beauty, is said to have been produced from the foam of the sea near the island *Cythera;* but, according to some, she was the daughter of Jupiter and the nymph Dione. She was the wife of Vulcan, but unfaithful to him, and licentious in the highest degree. Her worship was celebrated with the most disgraceful rites and ceremonies. The island of Cyprus was her favorite residence.

She is represented as a beautiful woman, richly attired, and girt about the waist with a cestus or zone, which had the power of inspiring love ; the Graces and Cupid attending her.

DIANA, the sister of Apollo, was the goddess of the woods and of hunting. She devoted herself to perpetual celibacy, and had for her attendants eighty nymphs, all of whom abjured the rites of marriage.

She is represented as a tall, majestic, and beautiful virgin, with a quiver on her shoulder,

and a javelin or bow in her right hand, cha-
sing deer, or other animals.

Ceres, the daughter of Saturn and Cybele,
and sister of Jupiter, was the goddess of corn
and harvest, and all the arts of agriculture.
She was the first who taught men to cultivate
the earth.   To her honors the celebrated Eleusinian Mysteries* were celebrated.

She is represented as a majestic and beautiful woman, her head crowned with ears of
corn, in one hand corn or poppies, and in the
other a lighted torch.

Vesta was the goddess of fire, and guardian
of houses and hearths.   She ever continued a
virgin.—She is represented in a long, flowing
robe, a veil on her head, a lamp in one hand,
and a javelin in the other.

The marine deities were Neptune and his
wife Amphitrite, Oceanus and his wife Thetys,
Triton, Proteus, Nereus, and his sister and wife
Doris, &c.

Neptune, the brother of Jupiter, was the god
of the sea, and second in rank among the gods.
Having conspired against Jupiter, he was banished from heaven, and for one year made subject to Laomedon, king of Troy, where he assisted to build the walls of that city.   He is represented seated in a chariot made of a sea-shell
drawn by sea-horses, surrounded by tritons,
nymphs, and sea-monsters.   On his head he

---

* See Grecian Antiquities, chap. v. sec. iv.

wears a crown, and in his hand holds a trident.

OCEANUS was the son of Cœlum and Terra, (that is, of Heaven and Earth.) He was called the father of gods and men, animals and rivers. He and his wife Thetys are said to have had three thousand sons.

TRITON was the son of Neptune and his wife Amphitrite; he was the herald and trumpeter of Neptune and Oceanus. Half of him resembles a man; the other part is like a fish; his feet are like those of a horse, his tail is cleft, and his hair resembles wild parsley. His trumpet is a large conch, or sea-shell.

PROTEUS, the son of Oceanus, could foretell future events, and change himself into any shape.

NEREUS, the son of Oceanus and Thetys, had also the faculty of assuming whatever form he pleased. By his wife Doris he was the father of fifty daughters called Nereids or Oceaniads, who were also water-deities.

The infernal deities were Pluto and his wife Proserpine, Plutus, Charon, the Furies, Fates, the three judges, Minos, Æacus, and Rhadamanthus.

PLUTO, the brother of Jupiter, was the king of the infernal regions. The goddesses all having refused to marry him, on account of his deformity and gloomy disposition, he seized Proserpine, the daughter of Ceres, in Sicily, and opening a passage through the earth, carried her to his residence, and made her queen of hell. No temples were erected to his honor.

He is represented seated on a throne of sulphur, from beneath which flow the rivers *Lethe*, *Phlegethon*, *Cocytus*, and *Acheron*. His countenance is stern ; on his head is a helmet ; in one hand a sceptre, or wand, and in the other, two keys. He is in an ebony chariot, drawn by four black horses.

PLUTUS was the god of riches. He was lame, blind, injudicious, and fearful. He is painted with wings, to signify the swiftness of his retreat when he departs.

CHARON was the ferryman of hell, an old man with gray hair, a long beard, filthy garments, and an ill-tempered disposition. Every ghost paid a small brass coin for his fare.

None could enter Charon's boat without a regular burial : without this they wandered a hundred years, amidst the mud and slime of the shore.

The FURIES were three in number, *Alecto*, *Tisiphone*, and *Megæra*. They have faces of women, eyes inflamed with wrath, with snakes twisted in their hair, holding in their hands torches, a whip, and chains. Their office was to punish the wicked. and torment their consciences.

The FATES were the daughters of Jupiter and Themis. Their names were *Atropos*, *Clotho*, and *Lachesis*. To them was intrusted the management of the thread of life ; *Clotho* held the distaff, *Lachesis* turned the wheel, and *Atropos* cut the thread. They were supposed to have absolute power, even over the gods.

Minos, Æacus, and Rhadamanthus were the three judges of the souls of the dead. They decreed various punishments to the wicked; and to the good they assigned a place in the delightful realms of Elysium.

There were innumerable other divinities of various characters and offices. A very few of these only can be here described.

Cupid, the son of Mars and Venus, was the god of love. He is represented as a beautiful winged boy, sometimes with a fillet over his eyes, a bow in his hand, and a quiver on his shoulders; sometimes with a torch in one hand, and in the other arrows or darts, with which he wounds the hearts of lovers. There was another *Cupid*, the son of Erebus and Nox.

The Graces or Charites were the daughters of Bacchus and Venus, and were three in number, *Aglaia*, *Thalia*, and *Euphrosyne*. By some they were said to be the daughters of Jupiter and Eurynome. To their influence was ascribed all that was pleasing, attractive, and *graceful* in nature and art. They are represented as young, blooming virgins, usually naked, to show their innocency, and holding each other by the hand, in token of their mutual affection.

The Muses, who were the goddesses of the

MYTHOLOGY. **305**

arts and sciences, music and poetry, were the daughters of Jupiter and Mnemosyne. They are generally represented with Apollo at their head. The palm-tree, the laurel, and many fountains, such as Hippocrene, Castalia, and the mountains Parnassus, Helicon, Pierus, and Pindus, which they inhabited, were sacred to them. The horse *Pegasus* generally grazed upon these mountains. The *Muses* were nine in number, viz:

1. CALLIOPE, who presided over eloquence and heroic poetry. She is represented as a young maid crowned with laurel, holding a trumpet in her right hand, and in her left a book.

2. CLIO, who presided over history, and is represented as Calliope, except sometimes she holds a *plectrum* or quill, with a lute.

3. ERATO, who presided over lyric and elegiac poetry, love-songs, and hymns. She is represented crowned with roses and myrtle, holding a lyre in her right hand, and a lute in her left.

4. EUTERPE, who presided over music, especially that of the flute. She is represented crowned with flowers, holding a flute and music papers in her hand.

5. POLYHYMNIA, who presided over singing and rhetoric, and was deemed the inventress of harmony. She is represented veiled in white, holding a sceptre in her left hand, and with her right hand raised up, as if ready to make

A A

a speech. She has a crown of jewels on her head.

6. MELPOMENE, who presided over tragedy. She is represented with a magnificent dress, wearing buskins, holding a dagger in one hand, and in the other a sceptre and crowns.

7. THALIA, who presided over pastorals and comedy. She is represented leaning on a column, holding a mask in her right hand, by which she is distinguished from her sisters.

8. TERPSICHORE, who presided over the harp and dancing. She is represented as a young virgin crowned with garlands, holding a harp in one hand, and surrounded with instruments of music.

9. URANIA, who presided over astronomy. She is represented dressed in an azure-colored robe, crowned with stars, holding a globe in her hands, and having many mathematical instruments placed around her.

Besides these, there were rural deities, as Pan, Sylvanus, Priapus, Terminus, Vertumnus, and others; there were also the Syrens, the Gorgons, Harpies, Dryades, Naiades, Nereides, &c.

PAN was the god of hunters, shepherds, fishermen, and of the mountains and country generally. He is represented as having two small horns on his head; his complexion was ruddy, his nose flat, and his legs, thighs, tail, and feet were those of a goat; he held a crook in one hand, and a pipe in the other.

Sylvanus presided over gardens and woods. He is generally represented holding a cypress in his hand.

Priapus was the tutelar deity of vineyards, orchards, and gardens. He is generally represented with a human face, and the ears of a goat; he holds a stick in his hand, with which he frightens away birds, a club to drive away thieves, and a scythe to prune the trees and cut down corn.

Terminus presided over land-marks and boundaries. He is represented with a human head, without feet or arms, to intimate that he never moved from the spot where he was placed.

Vertumnus presided over the spring and orchards. He had the power of assuming any shape. He is represented as a young man crowned with flowers, holding in his right hand fruit, and a crown of plenty in his left.

Flora or Chloris was the goddess of flowers and gardens. She is represented as crowned with flowers, and holding in her hand the horn of plenty.

Pomona was a nymph who presided over gardens, and was the goddess of all kinds of fruit-trees. She became the wife of Vertumnus.

Pales was the goddess of flocks, sheep-folds. and pastures. She is represented with a staff in her hand and a crown on her head, and was sometimes worshipped under trees instead of in temples.

Robigo or Rubigo was the goddess who preserved corn from blight.

The Fauns were rural deities, who inhabited the fields and formed a part of the train of Pan. They are represented as having the human figure, but with pointed ears and with the tail of a goat.

The Satyrs were also rural demi-gods, who chiefly attended upon Bacchus. They are represented like men, but with the feet and the legs of goats, short horns on the head, and the whole body covered with thick hair. They were sometimes called *Silvani*.

The Naiads were nymphs who presided over rivers, springs, wells, and fountains. They are represented as young and beautiful virgins, often leaning upon an urn, from which flows a stream of water.

The Dryads were nymphs who presided over the woods and forests.

The Hamadryades were nymphs who presided over trees. Every forest had its *Dryad*, and every tree its *Hamadryad*.

The Oreads were nymphs who presided over mountains.

The Limnads were nymphs who presided over lakes.

The Leimoniades were nymphs who presided over meadows.

The Potamids were nymphs who presided over rivers.

The Nereids were nymphs who presided over seas.

The Napææ were nymphs who presided over groves and vales.

The Nymphs were of two classes, terrestrial and marine. The sea or water-nymphs were called by the general name *Oceanides*. In these were included the *Nereids, Naiads,* Potamids, Limnads, &c.

The Tritons were sea-gods, with their upper parts like a man, and the lower parts resembling a fish.

The Sirens were sea-nymphs who had faces like women, and the lower parts of their bodies like fish. They had such melodious voices that mariners and voyagers were often allured by their songs to their own destruction, by being shipwrecked among the rocks which the Sirens inhabited.

The Gorgons were three sisters, *Stheno, Euryale,* and *Medusa,* all immortal except Medusa. They are represented as having their hair entwined with serpents, their hands made of brass, their wings the color of gold, their body covered with impenetrable scales, and their teeth long as the tusks of a wild boar. They had the power of turning into stones all those who looked at them.

The Harpies were three sisters, *Aello, Ocypete,* and *Celeno.* They were winged monsters with the faces of virgins, the ears of bears, the bodies of vultures, human arms and feet, with long sharp claws. They emitted an infectious smell, and polluted whatever they touched by their filth.

The LARES of the Romans were the *manes* (*i. e.* ghosts or shades) and images of their an cestors. Their PENATES were household gods, being images of such deities as were of divine origin.

URANUS or CŒLUS was the most ancient of all the gods. He was the father of Saturn.

SATURN was the god of time and father of Jupiter. He is represented as an old man, bent through age and infirmity. He holds a scythe in his right hand, with a serpent that bites its own tail, which is an emblem of time, and of the revolution of the year.

CYBELE, the wife of Saturn, was called the mother of the gods. She is the same as *Ops, Rhea, Bona Dea*, &c. She is represented as a robust woman, with rising turrets on her head, keys in her hand. Sometimes she is riding in a chariot drawn by two tame lions.

JANUS was the god of the year, and presided over the gates of heaven, and also over peace and war. His temple at Rome was open in time of war, and shut in time of peace. He is represented as having two faces, a key in his right hand, and a rod in his left.

BELLONA was the goddess of war and sister of Mars. She prepared his horses and chariot when he went to war. She is represented as holding a scourge in her hand, or a rod tinged with blood, with dishevelled hair and flaming eyes.

ÆOLUS was god of the winds and king of storms. He is represented as an old man with a long beard, holding a sceptre in his hand, sitting on a rock, or smiting the rock with his trident, at which signal the imprisoned winds rush out. Sometimes he is represented with a pair of bellows under his feet.

ÆSCULAPIUS was the god of medicine. He is represented with a large beard, holding a knotty staff, round which was entwined a serpent, the symbol of convalescence. Near him stands the cock, the symbol of watchfulness.

ASTRÆA was the goddess of justice. She is represented as a virgin, with a stern but majestic countenance. holding a pair of scales in one hand, and a sword in the other.

ATE was the goddess of evil. She raised such jealousy and sedition in heaven among the gods, that Jupiter banished her forever from heaven, and sent her to dwell on earth, where she incited mankind to wickedness, and sowed commotions among them. She is the same as *Discordia*.

AURORA was the goddess of the morning. She is represented as being drawn in a rose-colored chariot, and opening with her rosy fingers the gates of the east, pouring the dew upon the earth, and making the flowers grow -Her chariot is generally drawn by white horses, and she is covered with a veil.

BRIZO was the goddess of dreams, worshipped in Delos.

CARNA, or CARDINEA, was a goddess at Rome, who presided over hinges, and over the secret parts of the human body.

COMUS was the god of revelry, feasting, and nocturnal entertainments. He is represented as a youthful and intoxicated man, with a garland of flowers on his head and a torch in his hand, which seems to be falling.

CONCORDIA was the goddess of peace and concord at Rome. She is represented with wreaths of flowers on her head, and in one hand two horns of plenty, and in the other a bundle of rods, or a pomegranate.

COPIA was the goddess of plenty among the Romans. She is represented as bearing a horn filled with grapes, fruit, &c.

COTYS, or COTYTTO, was the goddess of debauchery.

FAMA was the goddess of report or rumor. She is represented with wings; with as many ears, eyes, and tongues, as feathers. She is said to fly through the world in the night, and in the day-time to look down from high towers and roofs: small at first, but gradually increasing in her progress.

FIDES was the goddess of faith, oaths, and honesty. She was represented with two hands joined close together.

FORTUNA was the goddess of fortune. She presided over riches and poverty, blessings and misfortunes, pleasures and pains. She was represented with a horn of plenty in her hands, being blindfolded, and holding a wheel as an emblem of her inconstancy.

GENIUS was the tutelary god who was supposed to preside over the actions, and to take care of every one from his birth to his death.

HARPOCRATES was the god of silence. He is represented as holding one of his fingers on his mouth.

HECATE was the goddess who presided over magic and enchantments. She was represented with three heads, or sometimes with three faces, with serpents hissing around her neck and shoulders.

HEBE, or JUVENTAS, was the goddess of youth. She was cup-bearer of the gods, and is represented with the cup in which she presents the nectar, under the figure of a charming young girl, her dress adorned with roses, and wearing a wreath of flowers.

The HORÆ were three sisters, *Eunomia*, *Dice*, and *Irene*. They presided over spring, summer, and winter.

HYGEIA, or HYIEA, was the goddess of health. She is represented as a maid of slender form, with a long, flowing robe. She has a bowl in her hand, from which a serpent is eating—an emblem of the medical art.

HYMENÆUS, or HYMEN, was the god of marriage. He is represented as having around his brows the flower of marjoram, in his left hand the flame-colored nuptial veil, in his right the nuptial torch, and on his feet, golden sandals.

LAVERNA was the goddess of thieves and robbers. She was represented by a head without a body.

LIBERTAS was the goddess of liberty. She was represented as a woman in a light dress, holding a rod in one hand and a cap in the other, both signs of independence, as the former was used by the magistrates in the manumission of slaves, and the latter was worn by slaves who were soon to be set at liberty.

LIBITINA was the goddess who presided over funerals.

LUCINA was the goddess who presided over the birth of children.

MOMUS was the god of mirth and pleasantry. He is represented raising a mask from his face, and holding a small figure in his hand.

MORS was one of the infernal deities, and presided over death. She was represented as a skeleton, clothed in a black garment, armed with a scythe and a cimeter.

MUTA was the goddess who presided over silence among the Romans.

NÆNIA was the goddess of lamentation, who was invoked at the funerals of the aged.

NEMESIS was one of the infernal deities, and the goddess of vengeance or retribution, always prepared to punish impiety, and at the same time liberally to reward the good and virtuous. She is represented under the figure of a majestic female, clothed in a tunic, a crown on her head, a cup in her left hand, and grasping her garments with her right.

VIRIPLACA was a goddess among the Romans, who presided over the peace of families. If any quarrel occurred between a man and his wife, they generally repaired to the temple of this goddess, and came back reconciled.

VERITAS was the goddess who presided over truth. She is represented as a young virgin, dressed in white apparel, with all the marks of youthful diffidence and modesty. She was sometimes said to hide herself at the bottom of a well, to intimate the difficulty with which she is found.

VACUNA was the goddess who presided over repose and leisure.

AUSTER presided over the south wind. He is represented as an old man with gray hair, a gloomy countenance, a head covered with clouds, a sable vesture, and dusky wings. He was the parent of rain.

BOREAS presided over the north wind. He is represented with wings and white hair, and always surrounded with impenetrable clouds.

EURUS presided over the southeast wind. He is represented as a young man, flying with great impetuosity, and often appearing in a playsome and wanton humor.

ZEPHYRUS presided over the west wind. He

is represented as young and gentle, and his lap is filled with vernal flowers.

Pitho was the goddess of persuasion. She is represented with a caduceus at her feet, as an emblem of persuasion.

Phobos or Terror was the god of terror. He was represented with a lion's head.

Somnus was one of the infernal deities, and presided over sleep. He is represented as sleeping on a bed of feathers, with black curtains.

Morpheus was also a god of sleep, but inferior to *Somnus*. He is represented as a sleeping child of great corpulence, and with wings. He holds a vase in one hand, and in the other some poppies.

Pax was the goddess of peace. She was represented with the horn of plenty, and carrying an olive branch in her hand.

There are many other deities mentioned by the classic authors, but these are the principal. The number of gods was increased by legislators, priests, and poets, till it became more than thirty thousand. These deities were supposed to mingle in the affairs of men, and were represented as being stained with almost every vice.

THE END.